Human Rights in Our Time

Also of Interest

†Available in hardcover and paperback.

About the Book and Editor

HUMAN RIGHTS IN OUR TIME
Essays in Memory of Victor Baras

edited by Marc F. Plattner

In the past decade, human rights as a component of U.S. foreign policy has been the subject of intense debate. First brought to the forefront by President Carter, it has also turned out to be one of the most controversial aspects of foreign policy during the Reagan administration. Policymakers who attempt to cope with human rights issues are immediately confronted with questions not only about the basic purposes of U.S. foreign policy, but also about the essential nature of our political system; they are compelled to reflect upon the interrelationship between domestic public opinion and the pursuit of U.S. interests abroad.

The complexity of human rights issues is reflected in the diverse contributions to this book. The authors examine the philosophical foundations of human rights, the lessons of history that are relevant to today's concerns, and contemporary policy. A concluding essay provides a critical analysis of the arguments made by the authors.

Dr. Marc F. Plattner, who is currently a fellow at the National Humanities Center in Research Triangle Park, North Carolina, served from 1981 to 1983 as an adviser on economic and social affairs with the U.S. Mission to the United Nations. He has also served as a program officer at the Twentieth Century Fund and as managing editor of *The Public Interest*. He is the author of *Rousseau's State of Nature* (1979) and of numerous articles and reviews on public policy issues.

Human Rights in Our Time
Essays in Memory of Victor Baras

edited by Marc F. Plattner

Westview Press • Boulder and London

Copyright © 1984 by Westview Press, Inc.

Published in 1984 in the United States of America by
Westview Press, Inc.
5500 Central Avenue
Boulder, Colorado 80301
Frederick A. Praeger, President and Publisher

Library of Congress Cataloging in Publication Data
Main entry under title:
Human rights in our time.
   Includes index.
   Contents: The philosophical foundation of human
rights / Clifford Orwin and Thomas Pangle–Human
rights and the international state system / Abram N.
Shulsky–The British campaign against the slave trade /
Charles H. Fairbanks, Jr., with Eli Nathans–[etc.]
   1. Civil rights–Addresses, essays, lectures.
2. Civil rights (International law)–Addresses, essays,
lectures.   3. United States–Foreign relations–
1977–   –Addresses, essays, lectures.   4. Baras,
Victor.   I. Baras, Victor.   II. Plattner, Marc F.,
1945–
K3240.6.H877   1983   323.4   83-19829
ISBN 0-86531-606-6

Printed and bound in the United States of America

5   4   3   2   1

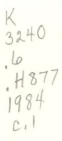
Contents

Preface

Although considerations of human rights have always been a factor in the foreign policy of the United States, it is only in the past decade that explicit discussion of the human rights issue has occupied the center of national debate. The story of this development is a complex one, but there can be no question about the central role of President Jimmy Carter in elevating human rights to the forefront of American consciousness. It was during the "human rights offensive" that marked the early years of the Carter administration that the work that culminated in this volume began. The contours of the human rights debate may have shifted somewhat since then, but it has lost none of its intensity. Indeed, no aspect of foreign policy has provoked greater controversy during the first part of the Reagan administration.

Among foreign policy issues, that of human rights is unique in the directness with which it raises theoretical questions of the most fundamental kind. The policymaker or critic who deals seriously with the problem of human rights is immediately confronted by questions not only about the basic purposes of U.S. foreign policy but also about the essential nature of the American regime. The issue of human rights compels us to pay particular attention to the point where foreign policy and domestic politics intersect; in a democratic and pluralistic country like the United States, the influence of domestic public opinion on foreign policy can hardly be overestimated. Moreover, now that the issue of human rights has gained a prominent place on the American political agenda, it powerfully affects the formulation of our foreign policy toward key countries and hence the details of our diplomacy as well.

The diversity of the essays that compose this book reflects the depth and the complexity of the subject of human rights. The volume begins with a study by Clifford Orwin and Thomas Pangle of the philosophical foundations of human rights. Next follow two essays that bring the lessons of history to bear on our current concerns with human rights: one by Abram N. Shulsky focusing on the seventeenth century and another by Charles H. Fairbanks, Jr., focusing on the nineteenth century. The four following essays, by Fred Baumann, Myron Rush, James Ring Adams, and Carnes Lord, deal more directly with questions of contemporary policy, but they too contain reflections of a more theoretical nature. Finally, in his concluding essay, James H. Nichols, Jr., takes on the difficult task of providing a critical analysis of the arguments offered by the other contributors.

Although there are some profound disagreements among the authors, it will undoubtedly be apparent to the discerning reader that they share a common perspective. They all possess a similar understanding of and devotion to the founding principles of the United States—principles that derive from the liberal political philosophy of thinkers such as Locke and Montesquieu. They all have a keen appreciation of the importance of ideas in politics. Yet they all remain no less aware of the recalcitrance of political reality to the noblest human conceptions and aspirations. These essays breathe a spirit of moderation that is equally divorced from both utopianism and cynicism.

This commonality of perspective is not accidental. The authors—and the editor—are all friends of long standing who have shared similar educations and who have helped to shape one another's views. There is also a more specific sense, however, in which this volume constitutes a work of friendship. The essays that follow have been written and collected as a tribute to the memory of another much beloved friend, Victor Baras, whose death in 1977 at the age of thirty-two left those who knew him with a sense of loss that time seems unable to heal.

Victor Baras received both a B.A. and a Ph.D. in government from Cornell University. Fred Baumann, Charles H. Fairbanks, Jr., Clifford Orwin, Thomas Pangle, and Abram Shulsky were all fellow under-graduates with Vic at Cornell. James Adams, Carnes Lord, James H. Nichols, Jr., and I were fellow graduate students. Myron Rush was Vic's thesis adviser and a teacher of all the other contributors as well.

Two memorial symposia devoted to the subject of human rights were held in Victor Baras's honor: The first took place in April 1978 at the New School for Social Research in New York City, where Vic was an assistant professor at the time of his death; and the second in October 1978 at Telluride House at Cornell, where Vic had lived as an under-graduate. Adams, Pangle, Rush, and Shulsky spoke at the New School symposium, and Baumann, Fairbanks, and Orwin at Telluride. The essays by these authors are extensive elaborations of their original presentations. The essays by Lord and Nichols were written especially for this volume.

The project of bringing all this material into publishable form was carried out under the sponsorship of the Salvatori Center for the Study of Individual Freedom at Claremont McKenna College, which was supported in this effort by a grant from the Institute for Educational Affairs. The authors and the editor extend their thanks to all these institutions, as well as to Thomas Main, who first brought this project to the attention of Westview Press.

In Victor Baras's all-too-brief academic career—three years of teaching at Wellesley and two years at the New School—he had already shown himself to be a fine scholar, a gifted writer, and a superb teacher. His articles and reviews had appeared not only in scholarly publications like *Slavic Studies* but also in intellectual journals such as *Commentary* and the *American Spectator*. His classes overflowed with students eager to listen to and debate with him. Vic's academic field of specialization was the politics of the Soviet Union and Eastern Europe, but his interests were wide and his learning was vast. Instead of the standard course in comparative politics, Vic characteristically taught a course that compared the regimes of ancient Athens and Sparta, the France of Louis XIV, Nazi Germany, and the Soviet Union; the reading list for his course ranged from Aristotle and Plutarch to the works of contemporary political science.

Human rights was a subject with which Victor Baras was deeply concerned—as an expert on the Soviet bloc, as a student of political philosophy, and as a man devoted to the political freedom that he and his immigrant parents had found in the United States. We believe that he would have regarded a book of essays on this subject as a fitting memorial. We hope that the contents of this volume display some measure of the theoretical insight, breadth of outlook, and political acumen that were so happily united in our friend Victor Baras.

Marc F. Plattner

About the Contributors

Thomas Pangle, associate professor of political economy at the University of Toronto, is the author of *Montesquieu's Philosophy of Liberalism* and of a translation, with an interpretive essay, of *Plato's Laws*.

Clifford Orwin is an associate professor of political economy at the University of Toronto. His articles have appeared in the *American Political Science Review*, *Political Theory*, the *American Scholar*, and the *Public Interest*.

†**Abram N. Shulsky** has taught political science at Cornell, Boston College, and Catholic University and has served as minority staff director of the Select Committee on Intelligence of the U.S. Senate. He currently works for the Department of Defense.

†**Charles H. Fairbanks, Jr.**, deputy assistant secretary of state for human rights, has also served as a member of the Policy Planning Staff of the State Department. Prior to entering government service, he was an associate professor of political science at Yale University.

Eli Nathans, a graduate of Yale and Oxford universities, is now a student at Harvard Law School.

Fred Baumann is assistant professor of political science at Kenyon College and director of the Public Affairs Conference Center at Kenyon.

Myron Rush is professor of government at Cornell University and author of *Political Succession in the USSR*, *Strategic Power and Soviet Foreign Policy* (with Arnold L. Horelick), and other books on Soviet politics.

James Ring Adams is a member of the Editorial Board of the *Wall Street Journal*, for which he has written a number of editorials on human rights issues. He is the author of the forthcoming book *Secrets of the Tax Revolt*.

†**Carnes Lord** is on the staff of the National Security Council. Formerly an assistant professor of government at the University of Virginia, he is the author of *Education and Culture in the Political Thought of Aristotle.*

James H. Nichols, Jr., is associate professor of political science at Claremont McKenna College, where he is also a research associate at the Salvatori Center for the Study of Individual Freedom. He is the author of *Epicurean Political Philosophy.*

Marc F. Plattner, who is currently a fellow at the National Humanities Center, served from 1981 to 1983 as adviser on economic and social affairs at the U.S. Mission to the United Nations. He is the author of *Rousseau's State of Nature* and numerous articles on public policy issues.

---

†The work of these contributors, which was substantially completed before they entered government service, reflects solely their own views and not necessarily those of the government agencies by which they are employed.

1

The Philosophical Foundation of Human Rights

Clifford Orwin and Thomas Pangle

Only in the West and in lands that it has touched, and only since the seventeenth century, has politics been understood as grounded upon rights enjoyed equally by all human beings simply because they are human beings. What once represented a novel transformation of the traditional Western understanding has become a Western imposition upon traditional understandings everywhere. One must at least wonder, however, whether in the course of conquering the world, "human rights" has not lost its soul. There is not a regime in the world today that does not profess to respect human rights. Yet there is hardly any political leader, sensible or otherwise, who can still articulate with confidence just what "human rights" means.

Part of the confusion over human rights stems from the very vogue the conception enjoys. Anything so prated about through all the nations of the earth is bound to lose much of its pristine core of meaning. It is also the case that regimes accused of violating human rights have a penchant for redefining those rights so as to bring themselves into compliance. The Soviet Union affirms human rights to those things that the Soviet Union already provides—like nominally universal access to free bad dental care. A great many Muhammads have taken this tempting shortcut to the mountain, and the clarity, as well as the reputation, of human rights has suffered as a result.

But political inconsistency and hypocrisy account for only a part of the confusion over human rights. Looming behind them is a problem of a more theoretical sort. In order to say what we mean by human rights, we must know what we mean by "human." By human, in turn, we must mean more than "born of human parents." Even if this last

---

This essay was originally published in the Fall 1982 issue of *This World*. Republished with permission. This version has been slightly revised.

definition were not tautological and did not presume a prior understanding of the term to be defined, it would still do no more than identify that class of beings that enjoys human rights. It can cast no light on the character of those rights. If we as human beings enjoy certain rights that other classes of beings do not, that is because human beings are beings of a certain kind. A human being understood one way, as our Founding Fathers did, for example, will appear to possess different human rights than would a human being understood differently—say as Plato, or the Stoics, did. As it is not overwhelmingly obvious in precisely what humanity consists, so it must be at least provisionally problematic in what human rights consist. In our century this problem has been vastly enlarged by the impact of modes of thought—especially Marxism, Existentialism, and certain types of scientism or behavioralism—that deny the possibility of speaking meaningfully of human nature at all. If man as a subject of rights is merely the product of ever-changing historical and cultural conditions, if he is nothing more than the malleable matter of an endless process of transformation, then there is nothing in him that can serve as the needed fixed star for "human rights." There can be no rational or permanent standard by which to guide our growing power for self-transformation and self-destruction and nothing in us that can claim exemption from social engineering and manipulation. The dramatic loss of clear focus in contemporary discourse about human rights is thus a fact of far more than academic interest. The malaise it engenders has spread to every battleground of the struggle for human rights. It helps explain why the West can be so vacillating in demanding or defending the rights that it has lived by these several centuries.

In what follows we try to contribute to a recovery of the lucidity and precision with which liberals once spoke of the "rights of man." With an outline of the authentic human rights tradition in view, we shall then briefly consider some of the current dilemmas we confront as heirs to this once young and vigorous tradition.

The notion of human rights, the appeal to the rights of man, stems from a specific tradition of political philosophy that began with Spinoza and Hobbes and matured in the writings of Locke, Montesquieu, Rousseau, and Kant. These men were the first to teach that all legitimate government derives its authority solely from the consent of the governed; that each sane adult, as an independent individual, must be understood to possess certain claims or rights that cannot be taken away, and for which he is beholden to no human authority; that far from being indebted to government or political society for these rights, the individual has joined with other individuals in creating, transforming, or maintaining government as an instrument whose major purpose is to protect and foster preexisting rights.

To grasp the significance of this point of departure, one must recall that prior to Thomas Hobbes, discussion of the legitimacy of government, or appeals to standards of good government, made almost no reference to rights that were not derivative from a person's duties as a citizen. An individual's political dignity was thought to be grounded in his belonging to larger social and political wholes of which he was necessarily a part. Titles to rule depended only partially on consent, and that consent did not create but merely recognized and ratified political authority grounded in other sources, such as divine revelation, age and experience, moral virtue, superior birth, wisdom, wealth, and parenthood. The purpose of authority so understood was to guide men to fulfillment through participation in a particular way of life that the community encouraged at the expense of other ways of life.

The commitment to human rights, however, does not entail an endorsement of any particular conception of human perfection or of man's destiny. On the contrary, to lay stress on the rights of man is to allow controversy about the ultimate meaning of life to recede into the background of politics. Government is certainly supposed to protect the "pursuit of happiness," but it should hesitate in giving direction to that pursuit; without becoming altogether neutral, or limitlessly tolerant, political life at its best is to foster a much greater diversity than was hitherto believed prudent or desirable. This wide shift in perspective follows from the insight that every human being, apart from and prior to any other ties and obligations he or she may have, possesses as an individual certain desires that are uniquely human and that cannot be chosen or rejected but are simply given. These desires are observably less alterable than any others and can therefore be said to be a part of man's natural constitution. The drive to satisfy them appears to be the only generally shared goal of human societies, and one may reasonably conclude that this drive is the fundamental and the only indisputable reason why men come together in political societies. It thus provides an objective political standard, a ground upon which all government, whatever its other aims, must stand—and which gives every citizen a set of claims against his government and his fellow citizens.

The Original Understanding

What are the desires that have such a status? The first and strongest, wrought into the very principles of human nature, is self-preservation. Nature teaches all creatures the general rule of self-preservation, but only in human beings does this rule operate through a potentially rational mind that produces knowledge of death and its causes, as well as a personality that seeks to sustain and continue to express itself. The mind's knowledge necessarily leads to anxiety and to an overwhelming urge to improve one's physical condition so as to postpone death and minimize the suffering that brings death nearer. Hence the root *human* need is, in Locke's phrase, "comfortable preservation,"[1] or what Montesquieu more expansively calls "that tranquillity of mind which arises from an individual's opinion of his security."[2] The basic raison d'être and responsibility of government is then not only to provide immediate physical security but also to give each individual the opportunity to make his own future more secure.

This means in the first place that individuals have a right to stable government that preserves order, outlaws violence on the part of private persons, and uses its own monopoly of coercion to protect citizens from assault on life or limb.

But it is not enough that citizens be kept merely alive and uninjured. Human beings have in the second place a right to liberty of action and movement that fosters their preservation by allowing them the expectation that the safety and comfort of their being and the continued exercise of their faculties do not depend on the arbitrary will of any other individual.

The action that is the most sensible response to the anxiety inherent in the human condition is productive labor, by which men transform the raw materials of nature into commodities of life. A crucial human freedom is therefore the freedom of labor and the freedom to enjoy the fruits of one's labor. But to provide much real security these fruits must be accumulable. It follows that men have, in the third place, a right to accumulate and use—even to destroy by using—outward things such as money, lands, houses, furniture, and the like. Without this, individuals in all stations of life lack firm trust that their own hard work will improve their condition; they lose the capacity to create tangible private barriers against ill fortune and the inevitable wearing down of all human conveniences; and it becomes much less likely that they can secure for themselves a permanent, private home—a sphere of their own within which to do as they please. The right to accumulate private property is hence at the heart of the original notion of human rights:

> Property being an inviolable and sacred right, no one may be deprived of it, except when the public necessity, legally established, evidently demands it, and under the condition of a just and prior indemnification.[3]

Given the incomprehension that so often attends contemporary discussion of the human right to property, it is perhaps prudent to pause and draw attention to what is distinctive about the understanding of property in this human rights tradition. For the idea of an inalienable right to acquire property stands in profound contrast to classical and medieval Christian or feudal conceptions. No longer is private property viewed as an uneasy, temporary compromise with human sinfulness or as the dangerous if necessary consequence of man's departure from the Age of Kronos, the Golden Age. Private property is now seen as an institution that gives reasonable expression to the need every man has to labor and coordinate his labor with that of others in order to ameliorate a natural situation of want and scarcity. The right of acquiring, and of enlarging one's acquisitions, may foster avarice and selfishness and may lead (especially when unregulated) to unfairness; but with all its failings, the system of private property can be at once an efficient incentive to the ever-increasing production that benefits all and a just recompense for differing degrees of mental and physical effort. Property so conceived is dynamic, not static, and its ownership and acquisition are to be diffused as widely as possible. There ceases to be any moral justification for restricting the ultimate control over land and material goods to a hierarchic minority purportedly endowed with superior virtue or wisdom, whether that wisdom has its source in nature, divine revelation, or insight into the "historical process."

Yet, as the famous pronouncement we have cited above indicates, the obligation of civil society to protect property by no means deprives government of the right and responsibility of regulating it. To quote John Locke, "In governments *the laws regulate* the right of property, and the possession of land is determined by positive constitutions"; men "enter into society with others for the securing *and regulating* of property."[4] Appropriate regulation of property ought to vary to suit the variety of geographic, historic, and economic circumstances. The regulation itself is a matter for prudence rather than strict rule or theoretical principle; in the words of Montesquieu, "There is nothing which is more in need of being guided by wisdom and prudence than the question of how much should be taken away and how much should be left in the hands of subjects."[5] It is thus altogether possible that a certain degree of socialism or government ownership may be compatible with the upholding of the right to private property.

Still, this "inviolable and sacred" right must never be lost sight of and must be viewed in the light of the differing and unequal laboring capacities of individuals. For the authors of *The Federalist Papers*, "the first object of government" is the "protection of these different and unequal faculties of acquiring property."[6] Or as Montesquieu puts it, "Let us then make it a maxim that when it comes to the public goods, the public good demands that one never deprive an individual of his goods, or rather that one take away from him the least possible."[7] The property right is obviously abridged whenever government ceases to maintain some opportunity for acquiring clear legal title, for saving and investment, for choice among investments, for moving about in quest of more lucrative, comfortable, or suitable work, for entering freely into enforceable contracts, and for organizing collective bargaining within the labor force.

The natural rights to life, liberty, and property gain an additional dimension from the fact that they flow not only from the desire for self-preservation but also from a second and different, though closely related, desire. Next to the desire for self-preservation there is planted in men by nature a strong desire of propagating their kind and continuing themselves in their posterity. We note that this human desire again represents a transformation of a drive that pervades all of life. All other creatures, one may say, have as their strongest desire the urge to propagate and continue their several *species;* but only human individuals can strive to continue their own *selves* in their offspring and come to love their offspring as an extension of themselves. This distinctively human relation to offspring, partly grounded in the equally distinctive human desire for self-preservation, is the universal—although not the sole—foundation of the human family, in all its varied manifestations. It is thus evident that the rights we are discussing inhere in human beings not only as individuals but as parents or potential parents concerned with protecting their children and spouses as well as themselves. To be sure, since the human family is permeated by convention and manifests itself in such manifold forms, many aspects of family life (including some of the most important ones) cannot be specified by the imperatives of human rights. Whether, for example, polygamy should be encouraged or forbidden; how contracts, divorce, and property between spouses should be regulated; the allowable sorts of population control: These are all affairs left to political prudence, religion, and moral tradition. What dedication to human rights does require is that legal authorities support the privacy and sanctity of the marital bond, the responsibility and authority of parents, and the honor and obedience owed by children. In particular, the rights of bequest and inheritance, as part of the fundamental property right, must be secured. For through bequeathal, parents may contribute personally to their children's future welfare while helping to insure that old age will find helpers eager to reciprocate the care and attention lavished upon them in their infancy.[8]

Political and Civil Rights

The principles outlined constitute the basic stratum of the human rights doctrine, but they are by themselves insufficient. In order to implement them, certain other rights must be established—rights that come into being through government or civil society and that are therefore called the "civil" and the "political" rights or liberties. It is useful to divide these into five levels, arranged in descending order of urgency.

On the first and most essential level are two rights without which it is impossible to envisage even a minimum of legitimacy in government, or any reliable safety for life and property: the right to emigrate and the right to the rule of law. Remove the former, and there is left no supposition that government is based on consent; accordingly, there can be left no great expectation that government heeds or respects the needs of the governed. In the absence of the latter—administration by standing, promulgated rules that apply generally and are enforced by known authorities who impose known penalties—citizens have no way of being sure what if any behavior will leave them free of menace from their governors and one another. Even foolish or brutal laws provide more protection than lawless authority.[9]

At the second level is the right to guarantees that the law, whatever it may be, will be enforced in an equitable manner, and that both public prosecutions and civil suits between private persons will be guided by fair and reasonable procedures. What this requires above all is a neutral and independent judiciary. The practices of such a judiciary may vary widely from one nation to another, but a small core of sacrosanct procedures can be specified—those minimally necessary to insure that both sides in a trial get a full and fair hearing. These include public and speedy trials that do not presume the guilt of the accused and that provide power of subpoena; access on the part of the accused to the charges, the witnesses, and the evidence against him or her, as well as access to counsel; and the prohibition of torture, coercion of witnesses, forced self-incrimination, and violation of marital confidentiality.

The third level of rights comprises the freedom to express one's opinions in speech and published writing. The primary justification for such freedom is the need men have to keep abreast of events within and without their societies in order to inform themselves and their rulers of threats to their security. Beyond this, economic growth (implicit in the property right) calls for a flow of information regarding trade, as well as the encouragement of technological research. But something more is at stake. Man's natural longings obviously are not circumscribed by the desire for comfortable self-preservation; one may also characterize man's right to liberty more broadly, as a right to the "pursuit of Happiness."[10] If the doctrine of the rights of men deduces universal rights principally from desires whose objects are universally agreed upon, it does not intend to deny other more spiritual longings the goals of which are doubtful or even highly controversial. We are not truly human without religious, artistic, and philosophic—as well as economic, political, and familial—expression. It follows that men have a right to a freedom of inquiry that goes beyond what may be required to promote domestic peace, economic growth, and national defense; men may demand, and given human nature, cannot but demand, that any legal restriction on speech be shown to be necessary for the maintenance of security and the prerequisites of a continuing exchange of ideas:

> No one should be disturbed because of his opinions, even religious, provided their manifestation does not disturb the public order established by law.

> The free communication of thoughts and opinions is one of the most precious rights of man; every citizen, therefore, may freely speak, write, and print, subject to responsibility for the abuse of that liberty in cases determined by law.[11]

The civil liberties enumerated thus far may persist in political systems that do not permit any further political role to the vast majority of the citizens; but even where these civil rights are well entrenched, men are quite reasonably uneasy about the future if they lack meaningful participation in the choice of the rulers who have the power to enforce or alter custom. At the fourth level, then, are the political rights of active citizenship in a government that is to some degree republican. The least this requires is that citizens have a right to representation in the legislative process, through delegates chosen in open and contested elections. As goes without saying, freedom of political speech, including protest and argument with government officials, is essential to this kind of political process. Furthermore, given the power of taxation to shape public policy and its potential threat to the property of the citizenry, representation will be genuinely significant only where the people's elected representatives have a decisive voice in the levying of taxes.

The foregoing remarks about republican government are of course highly abstract. If one attempts to move to more specific political prescriptions while still speaking the language of universal rights, one runs the risk of imposing a spurious homogeneity, and perhaps a dangerous straitjacket, on political prudence and cultural heterogeneity. Nevertheless, it is possible, proceeding with caution, to discern a fifth level of rights. Men have a right to a government that secures them against potential abuses of political power by distributing that power among distinct and balanced institutions or groups. The form this division of power takes may vary enormously, from the mixed regime of antiquity, through limited monarchy, to federalism and the bicameral legislature combined with separation of the legislative and executive functions. What is universal and simply human is only the right to protection through some such constitutional order.

The Kantian Transformation

It was in the name of this doctrine of human rights, elaborated by the giants of the Enlightenment, that glorious revolutions were fought and won in both England and America. But a long and important chapter in the philosophic understanding of human rights remained to be written, a chapter begun by Jean-Jacques Rousseau and completed by his successor Immanuel Kant. Although Kant adopted much of the human rights teaching of his great liberal predecessors, he was determined to place the teaching on a nobler footing. Inspired by Rousseau, Kant argued that man's assertion of his liberty cannot be convincingly accounted for wholly on the basis of the calculating desire for security; that may explain the genesis, but it cannot encompass the full power and meaning of the struggle for human rights. What is required in addition is some reflection on the historical unfolding of that struggle.[12] For in the course of history, as men have groped their way toward a deeper comprehension of freedom and of the institutions that best secure it, they have witnessed the awakening within mankind of a distinct and irreducible experience of reverence for the individual, as an autonomous, and not merely secure or comfortable, being. Men may begin by fighting for their rights largely in order to guarantee their safety; but in the process they discover that the rights are more precious than the safety the rights help secure. What is more, each person's attachment to his own rights is transformed by becoming subordinate to an attachment to the rights of men at large. Self-preservation comes to be seen as in the service of freedom, while freedom, and thereby life itself, takes on real dignity only when it is an expression of universal principles that can define the independence of all men as men. Paradoxically, by becoming partisans of the human rights, most if not all of whose content is dictated by the requirements of mundane security, men may discover the only genuine expression of a cosmopolitan humanity transcending mere security.

As men become self-conscious about this more sublime dimension of their commitment to the cause of human rights, they naturally seek opportunities to advance that cause throughout the world. In other words, when the human rights are seen from the perspective Kant identifies and promotes, the question of their *international* bearing comes increasingly to the fore. This question had always been present in discussions of the rights of man, but Kant tried to change both its formulation and the answer it received.

Initially, theorists of international relations who were influenced by the notion of natural rights tended to ascribe to the community of nations a much looser moral tie, and a weaker set of mutual policing duties, than had been advocated by the Christian natural law tradition. This last, with its doctrine of the "just war," its subordination of political concerns to theological ones, and its insistence on the unity of Christendom, had refused to acknowledge the moral self-sufficiency and hence the ultimate autonomy of any particular political community. Insofar, however, as government derives its purpose from the idea of human rights, it does not look to some cosmopolitan religious aim or to the promotion of some particular virtuous way of life in the world. Instead, it understands itself as dedicated to the protection of those citizens who consented to and created it and whose interests alone it "represents." With regard to other individuals or groups outside it, including other societies, each society remains in a "state of nature." It remains, that is, an independent or "sovereign" entity bound only by such obligations as it takes upon itself, in the form of treaties and the like. Each state is related to other states and persons in the same way that individuals are related to one another *prior* to contracting to form a society or submit to laws and government. Individuals in such a situation are concerned with the protection of the rights of others partly out of compassionate humanity, but mainly because they think an assault on another implies a threat to their own security. Once men live under the protective roof of government, the latter reason for being concerned about the rights of others who are not fellow inhabitants of the structure greatly diminishes. Each government, it is true, retains a vital concern for the independence and security of other governments, because an aggressor who menaces one nation may menace others—but concern for a neighbor government's independence does not seem to entail concern for the rights of individual subjects ruled by that government.

Yet it was recognized that there is some connection between any government's respect for the rights of its citizens and its belligerent or pacific proclivities. On the whole, it was thought, the more government is dedicated to providing security for its citizenry the less prone it is to be carried away by the religious, nationalist, and vainglorious enthusiasms that lead to war. Hence it makes good sense to cultivate concern for human rights among one's neighbors. But the most effective governmental means for doing so appeared to be the encouragement of international commerce, especially when conducted by private individuals. The free market gives rise to a relatively peaceful form of acquisitiveness or ambition and fosters enlightened, if selfish, impulses to property protection, freedom of movement and choice, and the exchange of ideas—including up-to-date ideas about legitimate government. Of course, these salutary results are less likely where trade is managed by government monopolies in tightly restricted economies.

This general outlook, which relies more on rightly understood self-interest than on humanitarianism, remains a defensible interpretation of the implications of human rights for foreign policy. But in the political philosophy of Kant a new understanding of the need for international *promotion* of human rights emerges. According to Kant, a necessary consequence of the progressive historical awakening of man's awareness of his human dignity (as an individual dedicated to universal rights) is a movement to educate and mobilize a public opinion that keeps vigilant watch over the fate of human rights in all corners of the globe.[13] Naturally, the question soon arises whether enlightened government should not be induced to lend its weight to such a movement. After all, government is a much more powerful advocate than any private individual or group; in addition, by publicly endorsing a more internationalist or cosmopolitan attitude toward human rights, government enhances the sanctity of these same rights within its own jurisdiction. The great difficulty, however, is this: The very same coercive strength that makes governmental suasion so compelling also poses a formidable threat to the self-determination of foreign peoples. If the commitment to human rights is intended to secure the conditions of autonomy, it ought not to risk depriving others of the challenge and the opportunity of deciding their own political destinies.

A League of Nations

What then ought to be done at the governmental level? The solution Kant proposes is international organization: the "League of Nations," for which he, more than any other philospher, provided the theoretical grounding. Kant rejected the idea of a true world government, and not only because he thought it impractical. He feared much more that the concentration of military force in one sovereign government would lead to a "soulless despotism" and the stifling of all meaningful diversity. That for which a liberal government should strive is a federation of nations, whose precise juridical status and powers Kant leaves tantalizingly ambiguous.[14] The federation's meetings could provide a neutral forum in which liberal governments might rally world opinion against violators of human rights. Even more important, Kant believed, was the progress a league of nations might make toward the goal of "Perpetual Peace." For it is through acts of war that governments engage in the most massive assaults on the security of individuals, and it is by having to go to war that individuals are compelled to treat others in ways that affront human rights most brutally. A confederacy of the states dedicated to peace and human rights could mitigate competition among members while bringing the weight of collective sanctions, including in the final analysis military sanctions, to bear against aggressors and nonliberal nations whose violations of human rights were so gross as to render internal resistance impossible.

Kant was aware that his elevating transformation of the human rights doctrine might render that doctrine more controversial. It was in his hands that human rights began to lose their moorings in indisputably evident, universally observable human desires and threatened to float up into the mists of metaphysical claims about free will, God, and the historical process. The most striking symptom is a change in terminology: Whereas Kant's forerunners spoke emphatically of human rights as "natural" rights—rights deducible from factual evidence of human practice—Kant initiates the tendency to eschew "empirical" evidence when speaking of the "normative" realm. Yet no political theorist was more anxious than Kant to provide norms for political action that would win universal acceptance from reasonable men. Kant therefore strove to prove that in the long run there was no conflict, that there was in fact a coincidence, between the demands of moral commitment to a League of Nations and the requirements of a purely pragmatic statecraft.

Although acknowledging that the spread of commerce and economic interdependence had the potential to pacify international competition, Kant pointed out that it hardly eliminated competition and, what was worse, armed that competition with financial and technological resources that made war more protracted and destructive when it did occur. By the same token, although Kant was even more hopeful than his predecessors that the imperatives of domestic economy and the spread of popular enlightenment would undermine oppressive government, he feared that the next few generations would see as much in the way of violent upheaval as of peaceful reform. What he predicted, therefore, was a growth in the ferocity and incidence of war stimulating an increasing awareness of war's folly. Eventually, a League of Nations with the liberal societies in the ascendant would cease to appear a utopian dream and become an irresistible demand of both political realism and popular sentiment.[15]

Kant's political thought, and the brand of liberal internationalism he engendered, evinces a remarkable mixture of lucidity and naivete. On the one hand, he was the first political philosopher to voice accurate, unmistakable warnings about the new dangers unleashed by weapons technology, economic centralization, and mass armies. On the other, his thought failed altogether to prepare men for an international situation riven by deep differences of principle or "ideology." Kant was under the illusion that such disputes were on the way to extinction along with religious warfare and "uncritical" metaphysics. The hopes he inspired for a League of Nations or a United Nations depended decisively on the emergence among the advanced or developed nations of a strong, unhypocritical consensus supporting human rights. That faith was sustainable so long as opposition seemed to come solely from the Right and could be labeled reactionary or atavistic. But the advent of a relentless left-wing totalitarianism claiming (with frightening plausibility) to represent the tide of history has shattered the Kantian dream. No sooner had "human rights" triumphed over the ancien regime—politically in the American and French Revolutions and spiritually in the minds of intellectuals almost everywhere in the West—than its pristine unity was rent, probably never to be restored.

For this outcome Kant himself must bear some of the responsibility. His understanding of human rights was at the same time moralistic and utopian: It held political life to moral standards of unprecedented rigor, while it preached—with qualifications that were almost sure to get lost in the shuffle—the imminence of an era of universal rationality and dignity. It thus aroused expectations that the older liberal understanding of human rights, and the societies grounded in it, could not and cannot hope to fulfill. Far from lending support to existing liberal regimes, the Kantian way of thinking about politics, especially in its Marxist and other left-wing transformations, has placed them permanently on the defensive.

At the same time it cannot be denied that Rousseau and Kant brought out the power of the moral appeal of human rights, an appeal that earlier theorists had exploited without sufficiently explaining. It is doubtful that the enthusiasm and even reverence commonly evoked by the doctrine of rights of man could ever have been due merely to enlightened self-interest. In particular, freedom of expression and the right to self-government shine with a dignity greater than that allowed for in the original version of the human rights teaching. Such freedoms must indeed be valued as means to securing each individual's pursuit of happiness defined primarily as safety and comfort, but at the same time they demand to be interpreted as expressions of humanity's spirituality. For this reason it is unlikely that any nation dedicated to human rights will permit its government to define "national interests" in purely expedient terms.

The Contemporary Crisis of Human Rights

Today we find ourselves in a situation for which the twofold philosophic tradition underlying human rights does not offer unambiguous guidance.

As a composite of different stages of Western thought, it is often at tension with itself, its two strands sustaining contradictory political conclusions. But far graver is the fact that the entire complex tradition has been superseded, in the predominant intellectual circles, by two newer understandings of politics that are hostile to the very notion of permanent, universal, and inviolable individual rights. One such understanding is Marxism, and the other is moral relativism.

If only for the sake of argument or because their opponents force them to it, Marxist and quasi-Marxist regimes have also taken to talking of human rights. For Marx himself, it must be noted, the rights of man offered a typically insidious example of "bourgeois formalism." They were the deceitful and self-deceiving veil behind which the bourgeois minority hid its exploitation of the proletarian majority. It is not only that these principles did not tend to the equal economic benefit of all—something, of course, that they had never pretended to do—but that they expressed, in their focus on the individual, an outmoded and perverted view of man. Self-concern, competitiveness, the family, and private property—all these must be dissolved in the cauldron of human "species-being" and by the abolition of the division of labor.

It is no wonder, then, that contemporary Marxist regimes greet criticism stated in terms of human rights with a collectivist reinterpretation of these that utterly transforms their original meaning. Sometimes, to be sure, they merely lie. Honoring the imposing example of Stalin's Constitution of 1935, they claim to extend to the individual a wide range of rights that they in fact deny him. Even in so lying, however, they assert that possession of such rights is contingent upon respect for collective interests. Insofar as Marxists will speak of sacrosanct human rights, they will vest them not in the individual but in the proletariat as a class, in the Marxist state, or the party—or, in the case of Third World pseudo-Marxists, in the popular or national will as divined by the nation's leaders. Rather than protecting the individual, "human rights" thus understood provide an unfailing excuse for ignoring and oppressing him. Hence that combination of surly contempt and aggrieved self-righteousness with which Marxist countries greet Western sallies in support of human rights.

The impact of moral (or historical or cultural) relativism on human rights is something to which we alluded in the first pages of this essay. Relativism makes human rights impossible in theory and so has confused and eroded commitment to them in practice. If there are no permanent, universal, and knowable standards of good or bad for human beings (whether founded, as Locke thought, in nature or, as Kant believed, in reason and history), there can be no authoritative enumeration of human rights. Like everything else in the moral realm, human rights become historically or culturally relative, or a matter of individual preference. No rational defense of human rights is possible, whether of the notion in general or of any particular version of it. This is a far cry from the "self-evident truths" that once presided over liberal democracy, as it is also from a Kantian faith in a rational historical process of which liberal society is the culmination. It means that however deeply we may happen to cherish our Western heritage of human rights, we have no rational ground for complaint if somebody thumbs his nose at them or is pleased to insist on an alternative list. For such a person rejects them with neither more nor less right than we cherish them.

Economic, Social, and Cultural Rights?

All of these confusions, and the diffidence stemming from them, converge on the issue of "economic, social, and cultural" rights. These are rights that, as their names imply, know how to keep their distance from civil and political ones. They include such things as a right to health, to housing, to education, to employment, and to many other goods. Separate United Nations covenants deal with each of these two "baskets" of rights, political and nonpolitical. This implicit recognition of the parity of the two has rightly been viewed as a victory for the Soviet Union as the patriarch of every society that underwrites, widely if not well, many of the rights just listed while quashing civil and political ones. Because there are now so many such societies, however, actual or merely aspiring, the victory is not that of the Russians alone, and it is no accident that in recent decades it has been this newer set of human rights that has tended to dominate international public discourse. The argument is often heard, and most of the nations of the world act as though they accept it, that nations must crawl before they can walk and that "economic, social, and cultural" rights are both more basic than, and a prerequisite of, civil and political ones.

At least as far as certain fundamental economic and social rights are concerned, there is some sense to this position. Nobody would deny that some degree of safety, health, and prosperity comprise the most urgent requirements of human beings. Nor may we doubt that civil and political freedoms will not long survive, nor easily come into being, where the longings for these basic goods are frustrated. Precisely because nobody would deny these things, however—least of all the founders of the original human rights tradition, so insistent on civil and political rights—we must attend to what may be lurking behind the current stress on these obvious points.

The notion of subpolitical rights is not in itself novel; Locke, it will be remembered, argued for natural rights to life, liberty, and property. What he meant by the last of these, however, was not a claim against society for any fixed degree of property, but the freedom or opportunity for all, within reasonable limits of law, to endeavor to acquire property and, having acquired it, to dispose of it. This right he presented as a natural and necessary extension of the right to endeavor to preserve oneself. And he went on to argue that in order for an individual to enjoy it in security, civil and political rights are required as well. Hence that venerable Lockean slogan, "no taxation without representation," which also implies the gamut of liberties needed to insure that representation is more than merely nominal.

In urging economic freedom for all under law as the crucial economic right, and in insisting on civil and political rights as its indispensable handmaidens, Locke articulated two of the cardinal premises of modern liberal democracy. He was also the proponent of a third, the truth of which has now been established for Western and non-Western societies alike: the efficacy of the combination of economic, civil, and political freedoms in fostering economic growth. In all of these respects, however, "economic rights" a la the United Nations present a rather different picture.

The ultimate primacy of economic concerns over political ones—the point of agreement between Locke and today's proponents of economic rights—is rarely used today as he used it, to argue vigorously for political rights. Instead the assumption seems to be that the two are commonly in tension and that the less-urgent political rights must wait—or be expressed only "collectively"—pending the achievement of "development." Economic needs serve to explain away, minimize, or detract attention from the widespread denial of political rights.

But are these economic goals properly awarded the honorific title "rights"? The striking fact is that today's fashionable "economic rights" are not necessarily either economic *freedoms* or economic claims *vested in each individual.* They are instead universal claims to the satisfaction of aggregate societal needs (housing, sanitation, education, etc.); as demands on the economy rather than rules for the protection of individuals, they lend themselves to justifying the suppression of economic freedoms and individual rights in the name of meeting the demands (or demonstrating statistical progress in meeting them). Moreover, the list of economic demands posing as ultimate, universal human rights tends to multiply, for no clear standard informs them, and no great reflection produced them. They are merely things that most people want, and that the poorer countries wish they could persuade the richer ones to give them. They are open-ended and hence often unreasonable. There is no way, for example, that an underdeveloped country can provide adequate education or medical care for all of its citizens. By proclaiming these as universal human rights, however, such countries arm themselves with the most respectable of reasons for pressing for the global redistribution of wealth. No one can blame them for that; but we can question the status as "human rights" of what are, in a sense, letters to Santa Claus. Meanwhile, it is sobering to observe that neither the United Nations International Covenant on Economic, Social, and Cultural Rights nor the Charter of Economic Rights and Duties of States so much as recognizes the individual's right to property or the state's duty to protect such a right.[16]

Right-wing regimes, to be sure, rarely succeed in dazzling the forums of international opinion by invoking collective and nonpolitical rights.

Right-wing collectivism is not much in demand. Besides, to liberals there is something transparent about citing economic freedom in defense of oligarchies that deliberately regulate property to prevent rather than to promote the diffusion of economic opportunity. But "progressive regimes"—one swallows hard at that term—by dint of their "progressiveness," do manage to fool a lot of the people a lot of the time, as they brandish many fine paper rights, primarily of the shiny, recently devised sort. It would be unpleasantly ironic if the rhetoric of human rights, having begun by staunchly propounding the freedoms of the individual, political and subpolitical, should come in the end to align itself against them.

The great practical achievement of the older human rights tradition, in establishing the "inalienable rights" of the individual, was precisely to deprive despotism of theoretical or philosophical respectability. There was no right, individual or collective, however derived, whether of a majority or minority, in the name of which any individual could be deprived of his rights unless he had voluntarily transferred or forfeited them. The newer tradition threatens to reverse this result. By transferring the focus of human rights away from the individual and his various freedoms, it takes the formerly inalienable and makes it hostage to other concerns. It has thus become easier to justify, harder to protect against, assaults upon the individual.

The Primacy of the Individual

We have already made it abundantly clear where we would turn to discover the theoretical foundation for a viable U.S. human rights policy. The place to begin is with the first and most basic—also by far the solidest—stratum of the modern human rights tradition. That is the one proclaimed by the Declaration of Independence and given its finest elaboration in the thoughtful rhetoric of Abraham Lincoln. More than any other, this aspect of the tradition is our own and remains embodied in the institutions of both our government and our society. It is the only version of human rights viable in the world today that focuses unequivocally on the individual and his basic freedoms. This is crucial in a world in which, as one careful surveyor of the state of human rights has concluded, "more and more the individual stands alone in the face of an all-pervading State."[17] If this focus on the individual can no longer bear, as it once seemed to do, the stamp of theoretical certainty, its practical urgency—and so, one may hope, its moral appeal—remains, to put it mildly, undiminished. Finally, this stratum of the human rights tradition is the least dogmatic or parochial and the most politic one.

This point is worth emphasizing. We are all used to hearing how the attempt to apply U.S. notions of human rights in milieux unreceptive to them smacks of naivete or even "cultural imperialism." Complacency and high-handedness do exist, and Americans have displayed their share of them. But the better we understand our tradition, the more it will

impress us by its inherent resilience and adaptability. To further the principles of human rights that underlie U.S. institutions is not necessarily to strive to export the institutions themselves, let alone to demand of other nations that they swallow them whole or as a whole. For these institutions are merely the adaptation, to conditions peculiar to the United States, of an understanding that originated in Europe and has become the common heritage of the West. To renew this understanding on the level of human rights policy need amount to nothing more parochial than this: to champion the cause of the priority, dignity, and liberties of the individual human being.

We have already suggested the relatively undogmatic character of that stratum of the human rights tradition that inspired the founders of the United States of America: By presenting this understanding in the form of a structure resembling a pyramid, we tried to indicate the order and relative priority of the different human rights. All the human rights merit protection, but not all are strictly absolute: What is required is respect for the edifice of human rights as a whole. Some rights are more urgent than others because the others depend on them, and their violation entails more lasting and destructive consequences. Thus any government may in a moment of crisis suspend civil and political liberties in order to maintain the prepolitical rights to life, private liberty, and property—such being also the only way of preserving the prospects of the liberties suspended. (Witness, even within the rights-loving Anglo-Saxon tradition, wartime censorship of the press and suspension of habeas corpus.)

Thus, also, verdicts as to the relative legitimacy of regimes in terms of human rights must attend not just to the rank of the rights that may be neglected, but to the rank and scope of such as may be protected. In such cases (it may be conceded) respect for the rights that are acknowledged will almost always suffer because of the neglect of those that are not: The different levels of rights, when in place, mutually reinforce one another. It may nonetheless be stated that in practice the protection of human rights need not be a matter of all or nothing. In addition, the concrete political situation and the viable alternatives open to the ruling body must be taken into account; nor is it merely the degree of the violation that is pertinent, but also its duration and the prospects for redress.

It follows that a reasonable policy of advancing human rights involves complex and cautious, if ultimately stern, moral judgment. It hardly helps to draw up lengthy lists of rights without indication of their justification, derivation, and ranking. This is another reason to be leery of the elaborate pronouncements of the United Nations, which prove to be less declarations of human rights than enumerations of ultimately desirable goals to be achieved universally in some world more fortunate than our own. When the permanent core of human rights is thus gift-wrapped in gossamer, the basic rights are obfuscated, their urgency

diluted. Indeed the very disproportion between utopian goals, propounded as absolute rights, and the capacity or willingness of most regimes to meet them is a loud and clear invitation to cynicism and hypocrisy. Where standards are hopelessly out of line, reality cuts them down to size, and the very notion of human rights is liable to fall into contempt.

It thus becomes important to gain greater clarity about the limits of what can properly be demanded in the name of human rights, and here we would emphasize two points. First, there is no human right to an equality of conditions, results, or outcomes in life. The idea of human rights implies that men are equal in a very precise sense: They are equal inasmuch as they are all endowed with the inalienable rights described above, and not in any other way.[18] What they make of life on the basis of these rights, together with their other distinct endowments (and what life makes of them), is not determined by the rights. The doctrine of human rights begins from awareness of, and strives to maintain respect for, human inequality and diversity; human rights are intended to foster the conditions within which individuality, creativity, and excellence can become manifest. None of this is to deny that a strong democratic bias is implicit in the political rights and the principle of government by consent. To quote Locke, there is to be "one Rule for Rich and Poor, for the Favourite at Court, and the Country Man at Plough"; for it is "the interest, as well as the intention of the People, to have a fair and *equal Representative*," by which means "every single person becomes subject, equally with other the meanest men, to those Laws, which he himself, as part of the Legislative has established."[19] This means that according to Locke's teaching political authority rests finally with the majority; but the distinguished or unusual individual and minority has as much right to the protection of life, liberty, and property from the tyranny of the majority as from any other tyranny—and the most astute philosophic schemes for balancing governmental power keep this right squarely in view.

The second point is really another aspect of this concern for individuality: Human rights belong to all people *as individuals*, not as members of any economic class, religion, race, or nation. Groups, other than the family, have no rights as such. "Group rights" are at most the expression of the rights of the individuals who comprise the groups, and no group may pursue its rights at the expense of the rights of any individual or any other group. One generation may not be forced to forego its rights for the sake of later generations or be deprived of its rights because of the supposed crimes of its forefathers; one class may not have its rights protected at the expense of another class's rights; an individual's belonging to any race or religion cannot disqualify him from equal protection of his rights; and so on.

From Principles to Policy

An intelligent application of the principles that we have expressed as a pyramid of rights would take note of those facts of life that currently surface under the names of collective, economic, and social rights. The fact is, such attention to harsh political realities is implicit in the principles themselves. Where a regime can make a powerful case for suspending or deferring less urgent rights for the sake of maintaining more urgent ones, we should hear it out, although not by any means uncritically. We should, accordingly, give credit where it is due to regimes that, unable for convincing reasons to implement the full range of human rights, display the most thorough commitment to those feasible under the circumstances. This we should do even where the rights protected are only subpolitical ones. We would not be true to our own tradition if we undervalued such solid goods as peace, order, and prosperity; economic and religious freedoms and the right to emigrate; the existence of an independent judiciary. At the same time neither would we be true to it if we did not insist on the incompleteness and precariousness of such goods where the other civil and political freedoms are lacking.

Here indeed our metaphor of the pyramid requires some correction. For it is not only the case that the lower freedoms must be present if the loftier ones are to be secured. The reverse is substantially true as well. Political and civic freedoms thus resemble the keystone of the arch of human rights. Comprising its highest point, they at the same time cement the whole, which without them must always threaten to collapse.

But besides emphasizing self-government as a means to securing subpolitical rights, we must also stress its intrinsic dignity. In this we would ratify in theory what has been amply established in practice: the extraordinary moral power of the appeal to political freedom. This, in other words, is the place to acknowledge the thought of Rousseau and Kant, with its emphasis on political freedom as a crucial aspect of moral freedom. In order to be satisfying, whether to ourselves or others, any human rights policy must attend to political rights not only as instrumental but as the culmination of the whole edifice—as neither the most urgent nor the least difficult, as the rarest but at the same time the finest rights of which human beings are capable. A unified and integrated structure of individual rights, worth preserving even when unfinished but achieving completeness only in free self-government limited by nothing but these rights themselves—such is the vision that we would offer over against the current ones. In short, we Americans should do whatever is feasible to reestablish ourselves as the party of freedom in the world.

The principles that we suggest represent a kind of synthesis of two successive stages of the Western human rights tradition, and a foreign policy informed by them would combine elements of the policies cor-

responding to each. Because, however, our synthesis of principle is an unequal one, drawing more heavily upon the cautious and flexible principles of the earlier human rights tradition, so too will the synthesis of policies be unequal. Just as every government is primarily responsible for protecting the human rights of its own citizens, the chief and overriding U.S. policy objective must remain the security of the United States—and such security cannot be maintained primarily by talk of human rights. Yet within the limits imposed upon it by this overriding objective, the United States should do its best to further human rights elsewhere in the world, relentlessly bringing the civil and political rights to the foreground of public attention.

Such a policy is all the more defensible in that the United States and its closest allies—Canada, Western Europe, Israel, Japan—which its own interest bids it defend, are also almost the only places where human rights, culminating in free self-government, have come into their own. The defense of the existing liberal democracies—and who can doubt that they are on the defensive?—is the real cornerstone of any grand strategy for the support of human rights. We must be clear on this: This is the cake; everything else, however worthy, is frosting.

But beyond this realm of our alliances, interest and principle are certain to diverge frequently, presenting policymakers with dilemmas that they will have to resolve as best they can. Because the countries that respect the whole range of human rights are so few, their defense will necessarily involve arrangements with countries that do not. It is now unfashionable to speak of the totality of anti-Communist nations as the "Free World," and in truth the "Free World" always harbored regimes to which freedom was only a euphemism. But if not all of the countries that belonged to the Free World were free, all of the free countries belonged to the Free World. So did most of the less free ones that were on the way to becoming freer. At some point it becomes necessary to weigh the exigencies of preserving human rights where they exist against those of extending them to places they do not.

Of such dilemmas there can be no theoretical resolution. Again we recall that, according to the original human rights understanding, national interest is by no means divorced from principle. The connections are two, however, and they may tend in opposite directions. On the one hand, a state is in principle a sovereign unit, and the primary obligations of its governors are to their own citizens and to their state's treaty allies. On the other, a state founded on the principles of human rights has also a powerful interest in the dissemination of those principles: There has never been a war between two liberal democracies. What is more, there can be no doubt that success at furthering human rights elsewhere would greatly boost the morale and prestige of the Western alliance—as failure to maintain them in any place where they presently exist would deliver a shattering blow to it.

With these considerations in mind, we have proposed a modified version of the original American human rights tradition as the one most

appropriate to the current situation. In theory our policy combines a commitment to the dignity of the individual with an appreciation of the other solid if less sublime blessings of the human rights tradition. In practice it encourages attention to the rank order of the various rights and to the exigencies of particular situations—encourages, but cannot insure; and this final point is worth stressing. For the human rights policy has not been invented that can substitute for the good sense of those called upon to implement it.

Notes

1. John Locke, *Two Treatises of Government* (New York: New American Library, 1965; originally published 1698), First Treatise, section 87.

2. Montesquieu, *The Spirit of the Laws*, Book 12, chapter 2, translated by the authors from *Oeuvres complètes de Montesquieu*, 2 vols., ed. Roger Caillois (Paris: Librairie Gallimard, Bibliothèque de la Pléiade, 1951; originally published 1748).

3. Declaration of the Rights of Man and Citizen (1789), Article 17; cf. Universal Declaration of Human Rights (1948), Article 17, section 1: "Everyone has the right to own property alone as well as in association with others," and section 2: "No one shall be arbitrarily deprived of his property."

4. Locke, *Two Treatises of Government*, Second Treatise, sections 50 and 120 (emphasis added); cf. William Blackstone *Commentaries on the Laws of England* (Chicago: University of Chicago Press, 1979; originally published 1765–69), Book 1, chapter 1, section 3.

5. Montesquieu, *The Spirit of the Laws*, Book 13, chapter 1.

6. *The Federalist Papers*, ed. Clinton Rossiter (New York: New American Library, 1961; originally published 1788), Paper 10.

7. Montesquieu, *The Spirit of the Laws*, Book 26, chapter 15.

8. Locke, *Two Treatises of Government*, First Treatise, sections 56 and 86–97; Second Treatise, sections 55–83; Blackstone, *Commentaries on the Laws of England*, Book 1, chapters 15–16; Montesquieu, *The Spirit of the Laws*, Book 6, chapter 20; Book 15, chapter 12; Book 26, chapters 3–6 and 14.

9. Cf. Blackstone, *Commentaries on the Laws of England*, Book 1, chapter 1, section 2.

10. Cf. Declaration of Independence (1776); and John Locke, *An Essay Concerning Human Understanding*, ed. Peter H. Nidditch (Oxford: Clarendon Press, 1979; originally published 1690), Book 2, chapter 31.

11. Declaration of the Rights of Man and Citizen, Articles 10 and 11.

12. Compare Jean-Jacques Rousseau, *The Social Contract* (Paris: Editions Garnier Frères, 1960; originally published 1762), Book 1, chapter 8, and *Discourse on the Origin of Inequality Among Men*, ed. and trans. Roger Masters (New York: St. Martin's Press, 1964), pp. 164–65, 178–79, with Immanuel Kant, "Idea for a Universal History from a Cosmopolitan Point of View" and "Conjectural Beginning of Human History," in *Kant on History*, ed. Lewis White Beck (Indianapolis: Bobbs-Merrill, 1963). For a fuller discussion of the theoretical background, see Thomas L. Pangle, "The Moral Basis of National Security: Four Historical Perspectives," in Klaus Knorr, ed., *Historical Dimensions of National Security Problems* (Lawrence, Kansas: University Press of Kansas, 1976), pp. 307–72.

13. Immanuel Kant, "An Old Question Raised Again: Is the Human Race Constantly Progressing?" in Beck, *Kant on History*.

14. Kant, "Idea for a Universal History," Sixth and Seventh Theses; "Perpetual Peace," in Beck, *Kant on History*, pp. 354–57, 367; "Theory and Practice," in *Kant's Political Writings*, ed Hans Reiss (Cambridge: Cambridge University Press, 1970), pp. 310–12; and "Conjectural Beginning of Human History," p. 121. (Page references to works of Kant are to the standard pagination keyed to the Königliche Preussischen Akademie der Wissenschaften edition.)

15. Kant, "Perpetual Peace," pp. 351, 368; "Idea for a Universal History," Seventh Thesis; "Theory and Practice," p. 311.

16. Contrast the United Nations Declaration on the Elimination of Discrimination Against Women (1967), Article 5, section 1, subsection a. The United Nations Declaration of the Rights of the Child (1959) upholds no right of the child to own any property, including a home, or to have any property held for the child by guardians; furthermore, it upholds no right of the child to have any precedence in inheriting the home or any of the property of the child's parents; contrast the enormously greater rights of children insisted on by Locke, *Two Treatises of Government*, First Treatise, sections 88–90. Observe, in this connection, the dilution of Article 17 of the Universal Declaration of Human Rights (1948) in Article 17 of the later United Nations International Covenant on Civil and Political Rights (compare Article 17 of the Declaration of the Rights of Man and Citizen [1789], quoted in the first pages of this chapter).

17. John P. Humphrey, "The International Law of Human Rights in the Middle Twentieth Century," in M. Box, ed., *The Present State of International Law and other Essays* (Kluwen, the Netherlands: 1973), p. 105.

18. Cf. Locke, *Two Treatises of Government*, Second Treatise, section 54.

19. Locke, *Two Treatises of Government*, Second Treatise, sections 94, 142, 158 (italics in the original).

2

Human Rights and the International State System

Abram N. Shulsky

The human rights campaign launched by the Carter administration raised a very basic question about the nature of the relations among states in the modern world. That campaign seemed to challenge the norms that have governed the international state system as it has evolved since the seventeenth century. This system postulates a number of independent sovereign states whose external relations are based on what we now call power politics, but whose internal affairs are solely the concern of each state itself and are not subject to interference by other states.

Viewed in this perspective, any attempt on our part to promote the enjoyment of human rights by the citizens of other countries appears as an illegitimate intrusion into those nations' internal affairs. It creates causes of conflict and dispute between other countries and ourselves where none need have existed and exacerbates preexisting tensions by introducing an additional bone of contention. By so doing it both hampers the pursuit of our own foreign policy, which ought to be based solely on our own national interests and hence ought not to spurn any foreign country whose friendship can be useful to us, and harms the general interest of all nations (including, of course, our own) in international peace and harmony.

The enshrinement in international law and practice of this system of independent sovereign states came after a long series of religious wars and disturbances, events that had effectively demonstrated the dangers of an international system in which seemingly irreconcilable religious differences formed the basis for equally irreconcilable political differences. The principle of the Treaty of Westphalia of 1648 (*cuius regio eius religio,* or, "whosesoever territory, his religion," that is, the ruler of each territory could determine the religious policies for that area without interference by anyone else) seemed to be a commonsensical and practical solution to a problem that otherwise appeared to defy resolution.

Is there any reason why an updated version of this doctrine is not equally applicable to our own time—"whosesoever territory, his ideology"? What "human rights" are, or whether they exist at all, is certainly an ideological question, and the Westphalian principle would therefore suggest that the observance (or nonobservance) of human rights is a matter for the competent authority in each country to decide for itself. In considering the applicability of this doctrine to the contemporary world, it will be helpful to examine why the principle of the Treaty of Westphalia was able to become the widely accepted basis of a new international system of independent and sovereign nation-states and thus was able to help put an end to almost a century and a half of warfare motivated, in substantial part, by religious differences.

What reasons may we adduce for this happy result? First of all, there was the fact of the simple exhaustion of the parties to the religious wars. The Thirty Years' War devastated a large part of central Europe and consumed the resources of the other European powers as well, so that there seemed to be no practical alternative to a policy of live and let live as far as religion was concerned. As long as the devastation remained vivid in people's minds, this basis of support for such a policy could also be expected to remain firm.

By analogy, it might be argued that a similar basis now exists for a policy of mutual toleration and accommodation on the part of liberal democracy and communism. Even though the clash between these two ideologies has not in fact produced devastation on a scale comparable to that of the Thirty Years' War, the widespread realization of the catastrophe that a nuclear World War III would bring should act as a more than adequate substitute. We have every possible reason for wanting to avoid such a clash, and, hence, we have every possible reason for advocating, it would seem, the mutual toleration that would make it less likely. From this perspective, raising the question of the violation of human rights in Communist countries would seem to be a reckless action, which only those who do not understand what it means to have multiple sovereign states in a nuclear-armed world could commit.

Still, we might wonder just how strong this incentive really is and just what restrictions on our behavior reasonably flow from it. The reasoning presented is, after all, similar to that which supports the Communist doctrine of "peaceful coexistence." At least in the post-Stalin period, official Soviet spokesmen have freely admitted that nuclear war would be a colossal disaster for all mankind, even if it ended, as they maintain, in a victory for socialism. Yet despite this recognition of the supreme importance of maintaining (nuclear) peace, the doctrine of "peaceful coexistence" envisages a continuing ideological struggle, leading eventually to the triumph of socialism. In fact, the relative security conferred by peaceful relations among the opposing camps makes possible a more vigorous ideological struggle, employing not only propaganda, but also political, economic, and even military support for pro-Communist groups in non-Communist countries.

In a similar vein, one strain of thought within the United States has argued against our imposing any "linkage" between issues of strategic relations such as arms control and any specific political or nonstrategic military actions by the Soviet Union. The paramount interest in preventing nuclear war is said to make it inappropriate to restrict actions that promise progress toward that end solely because of Soviet misbehavior in other, less important, areas. Although this lesson is never drawn by proponents of this viewpoint, the same reasoning should also lead the Soviets not to let our efforts on behalf of human rights affect strategic relations, thus enabling us to carry on the "ideological struggle" without jeopardizing our interest in avoiding nuclear war.

Power Politics vs. Ideology

A second reason for the success of the Westphalian principle was the persuasiveness of the notion of power politics as a sound and realistic basis for foreign policy. The central premise of the post-Westphalian paradigm of international relations is that the relationships among countries are governed by their "real" interests, as determined by economics, geography, and military technology, and not by their religious or ideological orientations. In other words, a country's foreign policy depends on abiding factors that would not be affected by a change in religion. Therefore, the major states no longer have any interest in the internal affairs of the other countries. Converting an important actor in the state system to one's own way of thinking about religious or ideological matters does not necessarily make that state an ally and hence does not necessarily change the international balance of power. Powerful evidence for this view emerged in the course of the Thirty Years' War itself, as Catholic France came to play an important role in sustaining the Protestant coalition against the Catholic Hapsburgs.

Does this paradigm adequately describe the present situation? A strong current of contemporary opinion claims that it does, and with a great deal of justification. The most obvious example is that of Communist China, whose ideologically motivated alliance with the Soviet Union was a relatively short-term affair. Current Chinese policy, driven by the ordinary maxims of power politics, has sought to improve relations with China's neighbor's neighbors (Western Europe) and with a remote and declining threat (the United States) as a means of fending off a close and growing one (the Soviet Union). Similarly, Yugoslavia, a Communist country, has relied for its security on the willingness of the Western countries to defend its independence from the Soviet Union. India, a fundamentally democratic country, has typically turned for support at critical moments in its foreign relations to the Soviet Union.

This viewpoint has considerable merit, especially as a necessary corrective to some simplistic ideological notions that may have had too much influence on U.S. foreign policy in past decades. But it would be going too far to claim that it accurately describes the political situation we face in the world today. In recent years, we have seen the development of what may be called the Soviet "mutual security system." When, for instance, the Soviets shifted their support from Somalia to Ethiopia in the course of the battles between those two countries over control of the Ogaden, it was perhaps possible to explain their action in terms of pure power politics—a Soviet desire to secure for themselves a more solid, lasting, and influential base of operations in the Horn of Africa. But when the Cubans followed suit, other motivations must have been at work.

Even more striking is the similar behavior of South Yemen, a member, along with Somalia, of the Arab League, which nevertheless was driven to favor the Ethiopians. This willingness to override the Arab nationalist impulse is clearly connected with South Yemen's membership in an ideological grouping. It would seem, then, that it does matter to us what the ideological affiliations of the countries of the world are, because those ideological affiliations do have a significant effect on foreign policy, even though they must compete for influence with nationalist impulses that are also present.

The same situation obtains with respect to the Communist parties of Western Europe, whose much-noted independence from Moscow does not seem inconsistent with a willingness to follow the twists and turns of Soviet policy outside the areas of their immediate concern, such as Eastern Europe. For example, the Italian Communists can see that a Soviet invasion of Poland would decrease their appeal in Italy, and they are not afraid to speak out against it, in the same manner as they criticized the Soviet invasion of Czechoslovakia. Yet when their immediate interests are not involved (as in the Horn of Africa), they show a greater willingness to be guided by ideological considerations.

In this connection, it is interesting to note that the Soviets have recently begun, in their relations with the Third World, to pay more attention to the "ideological purity" of their clients' regimes and the internal structure of their societies. The apparent Soviet complicity in the coups d'etat in South Yemen and Afghanistan in 1978, in which generally pro-Soviet leftist nationalist leaders were replaced by slavishly pro-Soviet Marxist-Leninists, suggests that the Soviets believe ideological orthodoxy will be effective in counteracting the natural tendency for national foreign policy goals to interfere with Communist ones.

The Enlightenment Perspective

The third and most important factor in the triumph of the Westphalian principle was a change in the intellectual climate that made it possible for religion to play a smaller and smaller role in international relations until it seemed to disappear as a factor altogether. The latter half of the seventeenth century and the eighteenth century saw the flowering of a philosophic school of thought that formed the basis of what we call the Enlightenment. In whatever other areas men might have required enlightening, it was certainly thought that, in practical terms, the most important was that of religion. This enlightenment could take several forms: Atheism, Deism, Latitudinarianism, or simply the belief in the preeminent importance of the mutual toleration of all religious sects. What these varying doctrinal positions had in common, however, was a tendency to remove religion from the questions on the public agenda.

To accomplish this, religious doctrines were either watered down to the point where they almost coincided with moral doctrine (and hence did not vary from sect to sect), or they were relegated to the realm of the private conscience of the individual. In this latter case, the test of purity and sincerity of belief became the extent to which the individual's private conscience is the sole arbiter, as well as the sole repository, of religious belief. Any attempt to impose this belief on others was deprived of all justification, because an imposed belief cannot, by definition, be a sincere one and therefore cannot have religious validity. Hence religious belief, either because of its weakness or its strength, was removed from the public arena, and it came to be regarded as pointless to fight about it.

By denying or rather attempting to minimize and abolish the political relevance of religion, the philosophic doctrines that underlie the Enlightenment sought to free men from unreal fears and disabuse them of vain hopes, in order that they might concentrate their attention on the real dangers and opportunities of their situation. These dangers consisted not of divine punishment or jealousy but rather of the "war of all against all" that constituted man's natural state. The solution to the "inconveniences" (to use Locke's understated characterization) of man's situation, was, again, not divine salvation but the human constitution of a governing authority able to keep peace among men and to allow them to pursue their own goals without harming others.

Just as man's misery in the natural state was not alleviated by any glimmer of divine justice or purpose, so his potential achievements in the political state were not limited by immutable divine superiority or jealousy. Man's origins were lower than had been thought, but his potential for achievement, individually and as a species, was much greater. The Enlightenment opened up the vista of a world of self-confident and self-sufficient men rationally pursuing their own well-being.

This perspective of the Enlightenment provided a ground on which Catholic and Protestant could meet. As a private, voluntary matter that dealt solely with spiritual questions, religion no longer needed to be a factor in international politics. International conflict continued, of course, but it could now be seen in the new light of "power politics": the struggle of states that, however much order they created internally among their own citizens, were still in a "state of nature" with respect to one another.

In the development of our own political thought, this liberating Enlightenment doctrine combined with older elements of the Western tradition, stemming from classical antiquity and the revealed religions, to produce a belief in the value of human freedom, not only as an efficacious and profitable organizing principle for society, but ultimately as something worth more than prosperity, security, or life itself. This philosophic basis has led to something of a paradox when it is applied to questions of foreign policy. On the one hand, it is considered to be of universal applicability, as it is based on "self-evident truths" that, as such, are valid for and accessible to all peoples at all times. On the other hand, it suggests that the United States is in a "state of nature" with respect to foreign countries and hence has neither motive nor pretext for promoting the cause of freedom within them. When Lincoln described the United States as the "last best hope of earth," he was asserting that the United States was the model for the development of other countries but that it could have an effect on them only by the power of its example.

Throughout the nineteenth century, the power of this example remained strong. No matter how many countries did not enjoy freedom, and however slow and tortuous the progress of many countries in the direction of freedom might be, history clearly seemed to be moving nations toward freedom rather than away from it. In this context, a free society might well feel that realism imposed strict limits on the amount and kind of aid that it could render to victims of tyranny in other countries.

The Totalitarian Challenge

There is reason to question, however, whether the policy embodied in Lincoln's description of the United States is adequate to the challenges of the twentieth century. For the twentieth century differs from the preceding ones in a very important respect: While tyranny is a disease of the body politic that is coeval with political life, it is only in the twentieth century that there has been a widespread willingness to overlook its evil nature when it appears in its modern totalitarian (Fascist or Communist) form. We face the fact that tyranny based on Communist ideology has demonstrated an ability to propagate itself in areas to which its tyrants' forces do not extend.

Leaving aside the sociological or economic causes of the attractiveness to some of Communist ideology, important though these causes undoubtedly are, we may note that this ideology itself is an outgrowth of that same Enlightenment in whose soil our own notion of human freedom has flourished. Indeed, it is in some respects a purer outgrowth. It is freer of premodern admixtures, and it is less reluctant, at least in theory, to accept the challenge of remolding the world, physical and social, to conform to manmade designs. Consequently, the Enlightenment, far from removing or softening the conflict between the competing ideological systems, as it did in the case of the competing religious systems, in fact serves as their battleground.

In the face of this situation, it is not surprising that attempts have been made to find or create a way of thinking that would bridge the gap between the two ideologies or at least would dampen the conflicts to which they give rise. One relatively straightforward effort to accomplish this was "convergence theory," according to which democracy and communism, under the pressure of objective circumstances (such as the requirements of a modern industrial economy), would both evolve toward a common ground of social democracy or democratic socialism. To the extent that this position was ever realistic, it reached its high-water mark in the spring of 1968 with the tremendous hopes that rode on the Czechoslovakian experiment in "socialism with a human face." The denouement of that drama seemed to demonstrate that there are substantial limits to the amount of convergence that is likely to take place in a quiet and peaceful manner.

A more subtle attempt to overcome the ideological divide has been made by those who place great emphasis on "global" or "North-South" issues. In a major foreign policy address at the beginning of his administration, President Carter stated his belief that North-South issues had now taken center stage from the older East-West ones. Such issues as the economic development of the Third World, the division of the "common" resources of the planet (for example, the resources of the deep seabed), and the prevention of major damage to the earth's environment (such as the depleting of the ozone layer) have the effect of minimizing the importance of the competing ideologies. If these issues ever gained sufficient salience and urgency, the result might be to dampen, or transcend, the ideological conflict as a feature of international relations. To date, however, they have had a small political effect in the West and none at all in the East.

Consequently, we must expect that the ideological competition between East and West, however subdued or genteel it may at times become, will remain a fundamental feature of international relations and that, in a sense, it will remain the highest stake for which the game of international politics is played. Although the realities of geography and military technology suggest that the game cannot be won, they also guarantee that it need not be lost. But the current stalemate should not mislead us into thinking that the basic differences have been resolved, or that, being unresolved, they can nevertheless fail to exert a critical influence on the course of world politics.

3

The British Campaign Against the Slave Trade

Charles H. Fairbanks, Jr.,
with Eli Nathans

In the aftermath of the Carter administration, there has been a wide-spread sense of the impossibility of continuing that administration's human rights policy, together with an uncertainty as to what might take its place. Any proposal for a human rights policy different from the Carter administration's must confront the serious case that may be made against carrying out any human rights policy at all. There are strong arguments against giving human rights a role as an explicit determinant of foreign policy. Some of the more important of these arguments may be briefly expressed as follows. First, it may be argued that no state will willingly accept interference in its internal affairs. Efforts to change the domestic habits of other states can only embitter them. A human rights campaign is therefore likely to increase international tension. More generally, the attempt to interfere in the internal affairs of other states would seem to destroy the only possible basis for harmony in international relations. States have a common "medium of exchange," through which they can deal with one another in a reasonable way, only in their foreign policy interests, which contradict one another but are of the same kind (power, prosperity, etc.). When, however, we turn from foreign policy goals external to the various human communities to their internal characters, we confront an irreducible diversity of political structures, cultures, and goals that provides no common basis for negotiation or cooperation.

Moreover, since human rights is a goal additional to the national interest, pursuing such a policy would seem inevitably to involve sacrificing the national interest in one way or another. A human rights policy may put the national interest at risk by creating unnecessary enmities with states that have different conceptions of human rights. It may undermine the power and legitimacy of allies in the attempt to change their human rights policies and make impossible detente with adversaries.

If, on the other hand, an attempt is made to avoid harming the national interest, other problems arise. One likely result is an inconsistent policy that oscillates between the orientations of human rights and national interest without satisfying either. Another consequence is that policy will appear hypocritical; the attempt to balance human rights and national-interest goals tends to suggest that the former are only a cloak for the latter.

A further difficulty for human rights policy arises over the fact that in most societies domestic concerns are taken far more seriously than relations with other states. A multitude of political communities have actually perished because they were unwilling to make the internal changes necessary to protect themselves against external threats: The U.S. experience with South Vietnam, for example, could be interpreted in this way. If this is the case, how likely is it that states will alter their domestic structure simply in order to satisfy the expectations of foreign countries pressing for human rights? Furthermore, diplomacy does not seem to be well adapted as an instrument to secure changes in domestic practices. The use or threat of force might appear more promising, but this seems to contradict the principled intent of a human rights policy.

Finally, it may be argued that even if a human rights policy can go so far as to produce changes in the organization of governments, it will not obtain the ends it seeks. The kind of human rights that exists in Western liberal democracies depends on a rare combination of political, economic, social, and cultural preconditions. Where these conditions are absent the effort to obtain human rights of the familiar kind is likely, while aiming at the impossible, to undermine the particular forms of decency that are possible. Such an effort risks sacrificing the real betterment of mankind for mere gestures.

These arguments combine to form a very serious indictment of any human rights policy. The case against having a human rights policy appears to be confirmed by the experience of this century. Carter's human rights policy did not achieve results commensurate with its resounding declarations and was partially abandoned in practice by the Carter administration itself. The other great international efforts for human rights in this century were those carried out by the Western liberal democracies after World War I, after World War II, and by setting up liberal-democratic regimes during the period of decolonization. None of these efforts remotely lived up to the expectations invested in them. After World War I, for example, more than ten new states and regimes were created in Central and Eastern Europe that were intended to embody the same principles of human rights that the Carter adminis-tration intended to advance. Within a few years all of these countries except Czechoslovakia had turned into Fascist or authoritarian regimes whose human rights practices were often worse than those of their predecessor regimes. Reflection on these problems suggests to many today that human rights should be discarded as a major focus of foreign policy and that we should return to strict *realpolitik* or national interest.

Arguments of this kind, and the examples adduced by them, are quite powerful. They suffer, however, from a lack of historical depth. The heroes of present-day advocates of *realpolitik* are mainly nineteenth-century statesmen such as Bismarck and Metternich. But the *realpolitik* practiced by such figures was not the *realpolitik* of fifteenth-century Italy, when the instruments of foreign policy included the convening of international conferences in order to kill the participants all at once. At the same time, the prevailing conception of human rights dictated that out-of-office reformers be burned at the stake. It is important to realize that the successful nineteenth-century practitioners of *realpolitik* operated within a framework that had not been set by *realpolitik*. In fact, they carried on foreign policy on the basis of the great movement for human rights that produced the modern West between the seventeenth and nineteenth centuries.

It is also true for us that any foreign policy, no matter how strictly its goals are confined to the national interest, works within a world constituted by previous human rights campaigns. We take for granted a world that is, in its political organization and moral assumptions, utterly different from the world of 1775, for example. The transformations have been so enormous that it would be wearisome to enumerate them, but the abolition of the legal inequalities based on class, ethnic group, and religion, including slavery, serfdom, and the privileges of the nobility, are among the most striking changes. These changes cannot have been merely the result of internal evolution; the mere fact that some countries (and those the most powerful) embodied modern conceptions of human rights before others was a force for imitation. In many cases it is an open fact that these changes were the result of direct pressure by foreign powers, that is, of human rights campaigns. In other words, if we look back as far as the nineteenth century, we see some human rights campaigns that appear to have been highly successful. It is important to look back at these instances to see whether we can learn anything about the conditions under which a human rights campaign can work effectively. The following discussion is intended as a study of one human rights campaign that was undoubtedly successful: the British campaign to get rid of the international slave trade in the nineteenth century.[1]

An Overview of British Policy

Popular agitation against slavery and the slave trade began in Britain late in the eighteenth century on the basis of new philosophic ideas about human rights. This effort achieved notable success by the first decade of the nineteenth century. In 1807 Parliament outlawed all slave trading by British subjects. Almost immediately thereafter the government began to press other countries to follow Britain's example. The campaign against the slave trade was to last more than two generations, peaking in midcentury and dying out as the traffic itself died out. The slave trade to Brazil and Cuba, the major nineteenth-century New World importers of slaves, was the chief focus of British pressure, but an effort was also made to stop the traffic between East Africa and Arabia and within Africa itself.

In a very short time Britain had been transformed from the biggest slave trader of the eighteenth century into a tremendous force to end the slave trade. This transformation was the direct consequence of the new philosophic ideas of human rights that had influenced the evolution of British politics during the eighteenth century and shaped the American and French revolutions. Britain's effort to end the slave trade was a human rights campaign not only in effect but also in origin and guiding impulse.

A few statistics will serve to indicate the magnitude and seriousness of the British human rights campaign. In 1846, at the height of the attack on the Brazilian slave trade, 25 of the navy's 239 ships and 2,967 of her 36,181 sailors were assigned to the West African squadron, whose principal function was to capture slavers. Three years later the navy, which had increased the West African squadron by 2 ships, placed an additional 6 ships on anti-slave-trade patrol off Brazil. British taxpayers spent an estimated £13,000,000 on the campaign against the Atlantic slave trade, much of it for naval patrols. The squadrons also cost the British dearly in lives; from 1830 until the end of the Atlantic slave trade in 1865, 1,687 sailors stationed off West Africa, the "white man's graveyard," died. Between 1810 and 1865 the navy seized 1,237 ships for engaging in slave trade, the vast majority of which were condemned as slavers, and freed 149,843 slaves, about 8 percent of the number estimated to have been successfully carried across the Atlantic. The campaign against the slave trade to Arabia was conducted on a smaller scale. From 1867 to 1878, the period of greatest British activity, the navy captured 348 slave dhows and liberated 6,367 slaves. The Arabian traffic died slowly, however, and Britain continued to fight it well into the twentieth century. The last slave dhow seized by Britain was taken in the Red Sea in 1923.

Britain's campaign against the slave trade was also serious in the sense that it was not a hypocritical manifestation of British self-interest. The relative role of "ideals" and "interest" in British action against slavery has been the subject of a long and complex scholarly debate. Perhaps the question is not clearly posed, as nineteenth-century liberal thinking, like the natural rights philosophy at its root, always insisted that self-interest and proper moral principles coincided at the deepest level. In any case, the historical evidence makes it clear that although some British interests benefited at certain times from abolition of the slave trade, the effort as a whole involved a considerable amount of inconvenience and sacrifice.

Planter interests in the West Indies and elsewhere opposed the legislation ending the slave trade to their plantations. Emancipation itself, which followed the prohibition of the slave trade, was a still more radical and unpopular measure. In 1833 Parliament ordered the liberation of slaves in those colonies settled by Europeans—the West Indies, South Africa, and Mauritius—and allocated £20,000,000 to be paid to their owners as compensation. A decade later Britain began the slow process of emancipating slaves in India. One of the more important manifestations of settler discontent occurred in South Africa. The abolition of slavery contributed to the decision of about half the Boer population to leave that country for the Transvaal and the Orange Free State, where they were free from British control (the "great trek" of 1834). In this case the effect of emancipation was to impoverish the Cape Colony and to create two intransigently hostile republics to the north that had to be conquered in 1898–1902 at a vast cost in lives and money.

There are two aspects of the British campaign against the slave trade that may cause us to question its seriousness. It was very slow to achieve its aims, and it did not deal directly with the root of the evil, slavery itself. Beginning after the Napoleonic Wars, it took Britain until 1851 to subdue the slave trade to Brazil. The effort to suppress the slave trade from Zanzibar to the Persian Gulf extended from 1821 to 1873. In these long years immense numbers of slaves passed into captivity or died on the slave ships. On this basis it could appear that Britain's efforts condoned injustice rather than opposing it in a forthright way.

We will consider later the possibility that Britain's aim was achieved so slowly because Britain adopted forceful methods of pressure only at the end. A number of historians believe that the methods used earlier—mutual search treaties and naval patrols—were not very effective. For a long time, on both sides of Africa, the British navy's efficiency in countering the slave trade resembled that of the U.S. border patrol in excluding Mexican laborers trying to enter the United States illegally. British opinion found it morally tolerable to diminish the evil without ending it at once.

The same attitude is visible in the British treatment of slavery itself. British aversion to the slave trade was based upon a wider and deeper aversion to slavery; no one had fought the slave trade before slavery itself began to be opposed. But for the bulk of the nineteenth century the British took action against slavery itself only within their own empire. All their international efforts were concentrated against the slave trade and not against slavery. This choice seems to have been based upon an awareness that slavery was far harder to abolish, because it was so deeply rooted in the social and economic life of independent countries and because it could not be attacked on the high seas as the slave trade could be. For these reasons, it was far easier to obtain an international consensus for the abolition of the slave trade than for any assault on slavery itself.

The choice not to fight slavery itself could be seen as arbitrary and opportunistic. But the historical fact seems to be that the abolition of the slave trade set the stage for the abolition of slavery, at least in Westernized countries and their colonies. The campaign against the slave trade weakened the economic basis of slavery. It established for the international community that slavery was so wrong as to be the object, in one of its aspects, of a determined attack. What the British seem to have done was to separate quite firmly the abuses of human rights that might yield to the means at their disposal and those that would not. They let the latter go, for the time being, while waging a very forceful campaign against the former. And they never let their attack on the slave trade be weakened by the realization that there was a more extensive evil they were not even tackling. These two features of British policy may have been essential to its success.

The Issue of International Law

The principal method Britain used to fight the slave trade was to seize ships engaged in the traffic. The use of this method ran up against international law. After 1808 the slave traders operated under the flags of nations other than Britain, and international law restricted the right to seize the merchant ships of other countries to countries at war with each other. Even the right to search the ships of another country was by international law a right of war, allowed to belligerent powers as a means of protecting themselves against the shipping of contraband by neutral nations. In the latter part of the Napoleonic Wars Britain had in fact used its belligerent rights as a means of suppressing the slave trade of neutral powers (several slavers flying the U.S. flag were condemned) and enemy countries (France and the Netherlands). Even the harsh necessities of war did not make Britain forget her human rights aim. Some zealous British captains went so far as to seize a number of slavers flying the flag of Portugal, an ally. After the Napoleonic Wars, however, British courts stopped these unilateral seizures, even in cases where Britain was merely enforcing another country's laws against the slave trade. When the navy took a French slave ship in 1816, a judge of the High Court of Admiralty ruled that he could

> find no authority that gives the right of interruption to the navigation of the states in amity upon the High Seas, excepting that which the rights of war give to both belligerents against neutrals . . . if this right of war is to be imported into a state of peace [for the purpose of suppressing the slave trade] it must be done by convention.[2]

British governments thus had to turn to securing the instruments of their policy by treaty. Over the next fifty years the United Kingdom expended enormous energy on extracting from dozens of countries treaties giving Britain the right to search their vessels and to seize them if they were slavers. These treaties varied in details, but all outlawed the slave trade to citizens of the second country and gave each power the right to search ships of the other. This right to search was in practice exercised almost exclusively by British ships, because only Britain maintained an effective squadron off Africa. The treaties often provided for the establishment of tribunals composed of representatives of both powers to try captured ships.

It was not difficult for Britain to obtain treaties from countries that were weak and only marginally involved in the slave trade. Countries that had a greater stake, however, usually had to be coerced. Spain and Portugal both signed treaties only under intense diplomatic pressure and with financial compensation from Britain. Zanzibar provided the necessary cooperation after being threatened with a British blockade. When lesser powers proved unwilling to provide Britain with the rights it sought or did not fulfill treaty obligations in good faith, Britain, adopting a less rigorous approach to international law, sometimes simply seized their slave ships and tried them in British courts. The slave trade to Brazil ended only after the British navy began seizing slavers in Brazilian harbors and inland waters, forcing Brazil to crack down on the slave trade to protect its own sovereignty. As we will show later in more detail, willingness to coerce other nations seems to have been a precondition of Britain's effectiveness in ending the slave trade.

At the end of 1814 the Congress of Vienna met to negotiate a comprehensive international settlement after a quarter-century of war. The United Kingdom attempted to make the abandonment of the slave trade part of this comprehensive settlement. Of the countries at Vienna only France, Spain, and Portugal still played a significant part in the slave trade.[3] Since France had already agreed to abolish the traffic within five years, Spain and Portugal were the chief targets of British pressure. Lord Castlereagh, the British foreign secretary, urged them to follow France's example. When this proposal was rejected, Castlereagh suggested a world economic boycott of the produce of slave-trading states—to the obvious advantage of the British West Indies. Russia, Prussia, and Austria supported Castlereagh on this, as on other questions concerning the slave trade, but Castlereagh decided not to insist on a boycott over the strenuous objections of Spain and Portugal.

On the question of the slave trade the Congress agreed only to declare that the traffic was "repugnant to the principles of humanity and universal morality" and that "the public voice in all civilized countries calls aloud for its prompt suppression." The powers that owned colonies involved in the traffic acknowledged the "duty and necessity" of abolishing the trade as soon as possible, but no deadlines were set.[4] At subsequent great-power conferences at London (1816), Aix-la-Chapelle (1818), and Verona (1822), Britain sought unsuccessfully to put teeth into the Vienna declaration through international agreements allowing her to search the ships of other countries. At Aix-la-Chapelle, Britain offered to give other states protection from the Barbary pirates in return for an international mutual search treaty; the British admiralty protested against such a new commitment. France refused to accept a mutual search treaty, however, and even Russia raised objections, so the offer came to nothing. Russia, Prussia, and Austria eventually consented to sign a mutual search treaty with Britain in 1841.

An attempt was thus made to suppress human rights violations through multilateral action, as has been attempted in our time by the League of Nations, the United Nations, and other international bodies. This route proved to be far less successful than bilateral negotiation or the unilateral action of Great Britain. The most important contribution of the multilateral action of international congresses seems to have been the establishment, at the Congress of Vienna, of an internationally recognized principle that legitimized the unilateral actions of Great Britain against the slave trade.

The willingness of countries such as Great Britain and France to turn against the slave trade was not, of course, the greatest test for the crusade against it. Although important interests in these countries were hurt by abolition of the slave trade, the traffic was not central to their societies. On the other hand, the economy of the Portuguese empire, both in Africa and Brazil, was based on slavery and the slave trade. Brazil imported an estimated 38 percent—3,647,000—of all the slaves who crossed the Atlantic in the four centuries of the slave trade to the Americas. After 1810 approximately 60 percent—1,145,000—of the slaves imported into the New World went to Brazil. Brazil's major crops—sugar, coffee, and cotton—were all grown with slave labor, under conditions so brutal that a new supply of slaves was constantly needed to sustain the system. "The annual mortality on many sugar plantations is so great," wrote the British consul in the province of Bahia in 1827, "that unless their numbers were augmented from abroad the whole slave population would become extinct in the course of about twenty years; the proprietors act on the calculation that it is cheaper to buy male slaves than to rear Negro children."[5] The Portuguese colony of Angola also depended on the slave trade. By the seventeenth century the traffic had become Angola's only commercial activity and the source of four-fifths of its public revenues. Mozambique began to supply slaves to Brazil somewhat later, and there too the trade became the most successful branch of commerce and the administration's greatest source of income.

The Slave Trade to Brazil

Britain's efforts to end the slave trade to Brazil took place in the context of political and economic relationships in which Britain was the dominant power. The Portuguese king, Dom João, who fled Lisbon for Brazil after Napoleon invaded Portugal in 1807, relied on British arms to regain the Portuguese crown. In 1826, British troops intervened in Portugal to protect the government from rebels equipped by Spain.

Portugal's dependence on Britain had enabled Britain to obtain a favorable commercial position in the Portuguese empire. In February 1810, Dom João signed a fifteen-year treaty guaranteeing that the duty on imported British goods would not exceed 15 percent and that no other nation would receive a lower rate. The treaty confirmed the ancient British privilege in the Portuguese empire of appointing judges to try cases involving British subjects. Britain made a few quite unequal economic concessions in return. More significant was the British promise to help Portugal in several territorial disputes with France and Spain and never to recognize as sovereign of Portugal any prince who was not the legitimate heir of the house of Braganza.

Brazil, whose trade with England was twice that of Portugal, renewed the commercial treaty in 1827. The treaty ensured British economic domination of Brazil: As long as British goods could enter the country and tariff rates were not discriminatory, British commercial preeminence would enable it to edge out its competitors. The result was indeed a dominant position for Britain. In 1842, 51 percent of the total imports of the port of Rio de Janeiro came from Britain and its possessions. The £2,626,000 worth of goods Britain traded to Brazil in 1840 came to about 5 percent of British exports.

Only three weeks after the Act of Parliament abolishing the slave trade received royal assent, on 25 March 1807, the British minister to Portugal urged the Portuguese government to follow Britain's example, or at least to restrict its own slave trade. That appeal, made before Napoleon's invasion of Portugal, was rebuffed. The king of Portugal found it more difficult to resist British pressure after he fled to Brazil. In February 1810, in a treaty signed at the same time as the commercial agreement described above, Dom João agreed to adopt "the most efficacious measures for bringing about the gradual abolition of slave trade throughout the whole of his dominions."[6] Portuguese subjects were now allowed to participate in the slave trade only between different parts of the Portuguese empire. Five years later, in January 1815, with the Portuguese court still in Brazil and the British army in control of Portugal, the king agreed to limit the Portuguese slave trade to areas south of the equator (where most of it was in fact conducted). In return, Britain remitted the unpaid balance of a £600,000 loan, about half the loan, and paid Portugal another £300,000 as indemnities for Portuguese slave ships seized by the British navy during the Napoleonic Wars. Supplemental articles signed in 1817 gave both powers the right to search each other's ships, established joint commissions to try ships captured as slavers, and provided that the right of search would continue for fifteen years after Portugal abolished the slave trade—at some future unspecified date.

The secession of Brazil in 1822 created a still better opportunity for British pressure on Portugal and its rebellious colony. The Portuguese government claimed that Britain had a duty to help Portugal reconquer

Brazil by the terms of a 1661 treaty obliging Britain to "defend and protect all Conquests or Colonies belonging to the Crown of Portugal, against all his enemies, as well future as present."[7] Portugal alone certainly lacked the power to retake Brazil. The British government had no intention of conquering Brazil for Portugal; but it could play on Brazil's desperate desire for recognition of her independence. Brazilian leaders were convinced that recognition by Britain would open the door to world-wide acceptance and reduce the dangers of anarchy and division that threatened the country. Brazil's representative in London reported to the Brazilian prime minister that "with England's friendship we can snap our fingers at the rest of the world . . . it will not be necessary to go begging for recognition from any other power for all will wish our friendship." Accordingly the Brazilian foreign minister told the British envoy in Brazil that "we are ready to do anything, everything, within our power, even beyond what the commonest prudence would authorize to show how much we prize, how really we are desirous to obtain the friendship of England and her acknowledgment of our independence."[8] It emerges quite clearly that all subsequent Brazilian and Portuguese cooperation in the campaign against the slave trade was grounded on the enormous weight of Great Britain in world affairs.

Britain's price for recognition was high: abolition of the slave trade. In 1823 Canning instructed the British negotiator in Brazil to make clear to the new government that

> the whole difference as to the manner in which a close connection with the new government of Brazil would be viewed in this country depends upon the single consideration, whether that government shall or shall not have proclaimed the abolition of the slave trade.[9]

These instructions are testimony to Britain's real seriousness about its human rights policy. When the Brazilian government refused to consider abolition without a delay of four to eight years, negotiations dragged out for three years. The passage of time induced Canning to soften his position. In May 1824 the United States recognized the independence of Brazil—the first country to do so—and Britain wished to prevent an increase of U.S. influence in Brazil. In addition, the 1810 commercial treaty was due to expire in 1825, and commercial interests in England were pressing the government to guarantee their standing in Brazil. But by signing a new commercial treaty with the Brazilian government Britain would be recognizing Brazil as an independent country, thereby eliminating the basis of its leverage on the question of the slave trade. Under these constraints, Canning decided in 1826 to accept a Brazilian promise to abolish the slave trade in three years. Brazil agreed that

> at the expiration of three years . . . it shall not be lawful for the subjects of the Emperor of Brazil to be concerned in the carrying on of the African slave trade under any pretext or in any manner whatever and the carrying

on of such trade after that period by any person, subject of his Imperial Majesty, shall be deemed and treated as piracy.[10]

Brazil thus secured a delay, but only when coupled with extreme sanctions. Moreover, Brazil accepted as binding on it the 1815 and 1817 Anglo-Portuguese treaties, which gave Britain the right to search Brazilian slave ships. In August 1827, Brazil signed a new fifteen-year commercial treaty granting Britain the advantages it had enjoyed under the earlier treaty.

The Problem of Enforcement

The British negotiator in Brazil warned Canning that the slave-trade treaty was bound to be "in the highest degree unpopular"; it had been, he commented later, "ceded at our request in opposition to the views and wishes of the whole empire."[11] The treaty was the subject of much angry discussion in the Brazilian Chamber of Deputies, but as the emperor had the power to sign treaties on his own authority, the indignant reaction did not undo the negotiations.

During the grace period a record 175,000 slaves were poured into Brazil. When the three years had passed, the Brazilian government did decree that all slaves who entered the country after 1830 were legally free and established penalties for engaging in the slave trade. But the traffic soon revived. At the local level the administration of justice was dominated by landowning interests, and these officials usually cooperated willingly with efforts to evade the new laws. In January 1835 the president of Rio de Janeiro province complained to the minister of justice that, on the question of the slave trade, he was "almost reduced to the character of a mere spectator of crimes which I can neither check nor punish."[12] In 1835 and again in 1837 the Brazilian government proposed measures to the Chamber of Deputies that would have assisted Britain in fighting the slave trade more effectively, but the Chamber of Deputies refused to accept them. These proposals would have permitted the Anglo-Brazilian commissions that judged slaves to condemn slave ships that did not have slaves actually on board. The treaty of 1817, under which Britain had the right to search and seize Brazilian slavers, lacked such a clause, and this seriously interfered with the effectiveness of the British patrol. In the spring of 1838 a recent minister of justice and of foreign affairs in the Brazilian government described the universal disregard for the laws against the slave trade:

> The law of 7 November [1831—the measure that made slaves who entered the country after 1830 legally free] is a complete nullity. The object of putting a stop to the traffic has not been attained, nor have the government any hopes that it will be. The speculators in it rely on a total impunity the moment the landing is effected. Many of the local authorities protect the disembarkation of the slaves and their passage from one point to

another. In several places this is going on in the face of open day and
at any hour without concealment. Woe to the magistrate who should
attempt to interfere. He becomes an object of hatred, his life is in danger
and some have been assassinated. No captures are made at sea for the
promised reward is no longer paid to the captors. In a word, all conspire
in favor of the traffic and against the law to repress it.[13]

The effectiveness of Britain's campaign was thus curbed by her inability
to control domestic sentiment in Brazil. In addition, by narrowly defining
culpable slave ships as those that actually had slaves on board, Brazil
severely hampered the work of Britain's West African squadron. Nevertheless, the slave traders who supplied Brazil found the British navy
menacing enough to look for other colors after 1830. The Portuguese
flag offered more protection than Brazil's, and it quickly came to dominate
the slave trade to Brazil. The safety offered by the Portuguese flag
sprang from a deficiency (from the British point of view) in the 1817
treaty giving the right to search Portuguese slave ships. The treaty had
limited that right to areas north of the equator, and the law officers of
the British crown advised in 1830 and again in 1832 that Britain had
no right to seize Portuguese ships that were engaged in the slave trade
south of the equator, even if the destination of the slaves was clearly
outside the Portuguese empire. There repeatedly proved to be a tension
between British respect for law and the success of the campaign against
the slave trade.

Some change appeared likely in 1836 when a new Portuguese government banned the slave trade to Portuguese subjects in all areas,
although with a number of exceptions. British hopes were soon frustrated,
however. "Like all previous Portuguese anti-slave trade laws and decrees
it proved to be a dead letter from the start."[14] The governors of both
Angola and Mozambique suspended the law, claiming that it could not
be enforced and, if it were, it would ruin the colonies. British efforts
to persuade Portugal to sign an acceptable mutual search treaty came
close to success in 1836 and again in 1839 but fell through at the last
minute. The reason for the failure of negotiations in 1839 indicates the
nature of Portuguese anxieties; Portugal refused to sign when Britain
rejected a final demand for a promise of substantial land and sea support
if the treaty led to a revolt in Portugal's colonies.

During the unsuccessful Anglo-Portuguese negotiations of 1838, Lord
Palmerston, the foreign secretary, had ordered the British negotiator to
make clear to the Portuguese that if Portugal continued to balk at a
mutual search treaty, Britain would take "what the Americans call high-
handed measures" and "deal unceremoniously" with the Portuguese
flag.[15] Palmerston's private letters to the British envoy show that he
had considered and accepted the risk that Portugal would fight back.
If Portugal chose to declare war, he wrote, "so much the better. . . .
There are several of her colonies which would suit us remarkably well,
and having taken them in war we should retain them at the peace

which she would beg on her knees to obtain from us." A later letter is even more menacing: "We cannot class Portugal among the powers with which England is on terms of friendly alliance. We consider Portugal as morally at war with us and if she does not take good care and look well ahead she will be physically at war with us also."[16]

When the talks broke down in February 1839, Palmerston acted on his threats. Alleging that Portugal had failed in good faith to live up to the commitment it had made in 1810 to adopt "the most efficacious measures for bringing about the abolition of the slave trade" or to the commitment it made in 1815 to limit the slave trade conducted by its citizens to Portuguese possessions, Palmerston claimed the right to resort to unilateral seizures of Portuguese ships.[17] On 10 July 1839 he introduced a bill into the House of Commons empowering the navy to seize Portuguese slave ships and British admiralty courts to try them. Under this bill the presence of slaving equipment was sufficient grounds for condemnation. Lord Peel, the leader of the Tory opposition in the House of Commons, felt the bill was entirely justified, and it passed Commons without a debate. In the House of Lords, however, the duke of Wellington successfully opposed it. He argued that the bill was contrary to international law, since Britain claimed the right of search without the explicit approval of the nation whose ships were involved. He also raised a constitutional objection: If Britain were to make war on Portugal, the executive rather than the legislature should take responsibility. Wellington prevailed by a 38–32 vote. A week later Palmerston introduced a similar bill that made it clear that the executive was taking the initiative and that parliamentary approval was needed chiefly to protect individual British officers against suits by private Portuguese who had suffered injury. Wellington continued his opposition, but the bill passed the House of Lords by a 39–38 vote, and in September orders were given to British officers to capture Portuguese slavers and send them to British vice-admiralty courts. The successful British human rights campaign thus differed from Jimmy Carter's in not being conjoined with a noninterventionist foreign policy. Great Britain did not renounce the use of force or shrink from imposing its own conception of morality on other nations.

The year 1839 also saw an increase in the effectiveness of the West African squadron against ships flying the Brazilian flag (to which Portuguese slavers had begun to return during the summer of 1839). In that year, using tortured legal reasoning, the British judges on the Anglo-Brazilian commissions discovered the authority to condemn slavers captured without slaves but with slaving equipment. Palmerston promptly accepted this gift, despite the legal qualms of the British advocate general, and ordered the British fleet to make use of its new powers. The Brazilian members of the commissions did not, as a rule, accept the new interpretation. But the British brought almost all of the slavers they captured to Sierra Leone, on the West coast of Africa. The commissions sitting there usually lacked a full contingent of Brazilian judges, and the British interpretation thus prevailed. Convictions were much harder to obtain in Rio de Janiero, where the Brazilians made sure to have full representation.

The "high-handed" turn of British policy in 1839 opened "an era in the history of the slave trade when for the first time suppression became possible," as Captain Joseph Denman, an officer in the West African squadron, testified in 1845.[18] There were no more cases like that of the *Maria da Gloria*, a slave ship taken in 1833. The *Maria da Gloria* crossed the Atlantic three times—with slaves on board—as its British captors sought unsuccessfully to have it convicted by Anglo-Brazilian and Anglo-Portuguese commissions. The ship returned to Brazil "a floating charnel house"; a quarter of its cargo died in the course of the ordeal.[19] Between 1830 and 1838 approximately 20 slave ships engaged in the trade to Brazil had been captured by the navy, but 150 were captured between 1839 and 1842. On a number of occasions in 1841 and 1842 British ships landed seamen in Africa to destroy slave depots, freeing over 2,000 slaves. Lord Palmerston commented that "taking a wasp's nest . . . is more effective than catching the wasps one by one."[20] The British also became much more aggressive off the Brazilian coast. In 1841 a British ship seized a Portuguese slaver inside Rio de Janeiro harbor and was fired on as it left the port. Small armed British boats cruised close to the Brazilian shore on anti–slave-trade patrol and were on a number of occasions attacked by angry slave traders and local authorities. In November 1841 the Whig government fell and the aggressive Palmerston was replaced at the foreign office by the more pacific Lord Aberdeen. The result was greater caution on the part of the British fleet. In 1842 Aberdeen ordered the navy to stop landing and destroying slave depots in Africa; in 1844 he ordered a halt to the seizure of slavers in Brazilian waters. Aberdeen also eased tensions with Portugal by signing a mutual search treaty in 1842, a treaty that gave Britain all the powers she wanted.

The Crushing of the Brazilian Slave Trade

In the struggle against the Brazilian slave trade, 1845 was a turning point. In that year Britain's right to search Brazilian ships under the 1817 treaty expired. That treaty had provided that the right of mutual search was to last for fifteen years following the abolition of the slave trade, and in 1845 the fifteen years were up. The Brazilian government had no intention of renewing the mutual search treaty. But even Lord Aberdeen would not let the British anti–slave-trade campaign end so ignominiously. In July 1845 he introduced a bill that treated Brazil as Portugal had been treated from 1839 to 1842. Aberdeen claimed that the clause of the 1826 treaty that declared that slave trading by Brazilian subjects "shall be deemed and treated as piracy" gave Britain the right to seize and try Brazilian slavers without supplementary treaties. Britain had simply not exercised its full rights during the previous fifteen years. A handful of members of Parliament opposed the bill out of concern over its effect on commerce with Brazil and its legality. But with the leadership of both parties behind it, the Aberdeen Act passed easily.

It is surprising to find among those who opposed the Aberdeen Act a number of abolitionists, some of them quite prominent. These were men who viewed the use of the navy to suppress the slave trade as both ineffective and unnecessarily warlike. The radical Quaker who founded the British and Foreign Anti-Slavery Society in 1839 believed that Britain should use "moral, religious, and pacific means" to abolish slavery and the slave trade, instead of "trying to promote philanthropic ends by violence and blood."[21] In 1845 Thomas Clarkson, then president of the British and Foreign Anti-Slavery Society, urged Lord Aberdeen to abandon existing policies and instead concentrate on "creating where it does not exist and fostering where they see germs of it a sense of humanity and moral rectitude."[22] Numerous other abolitionists, it should be noted, continued to support the government's policy. The success of Britain's campaign was dependent on the weakness of this type of pacifist sentiment.

The British navy proved unable to put an end to the Brazilian slave trade in the five years that followed the passage of the Aberdeen Act. This strengthened the hand of those who wanted to do away with the anti–slave-trade squadron. Although British ships seized a record 400 slavers engaged in the trade to Brazil between 1845 and 1850, the traffic flourished: Approximately 150,000 slaves were imported into Brazil from 1846 to 1849. The surge in slave imports was the result of increased foreign demand for Brazilian crops; in the second half of the 1840s coffee exports rose 40 percent over the first half of the decade. Sugar exports rose as well. Brazil's trade boom sprang in part from British policy, for in 1846 Parliament greatly lowered the earlier prohibitive tariff against foreign sugar, opening the British market to Brazil.

The prosperity of the slave trade precisely when the British navy was making its greatest efforts seemed to some clear evidence of the failure of the West African squadron. In March 1848, eighty members of the House of Commons voted for its withdrawal. A year later a Commons committee appointed to study the question also recommended, by a narrow margin, that the West African squadron be withdrawn. The final showdown came in March 1850, when Commons again voted on whether to continue using the navy as a means of abolishing the slave trade. Many newspapers had joined the opponents of the squadron. According to the *Times* the government's policy was "stupendous folly," and the *Morning Chronicle* called it "a cruel, hopeless, and absurd experiment." The abolitionist movement, which had suffered something of a decline in popular support, split on the question. Lord Russell, the prime minister, was anxious and warned a meeting of Whigs the night before the vote that he and Palmerston would resign if Commons recalled the squadron—a threat that showed how seriously British leaders took their campaign. The government won, but by the uncomfortably small margin of 232 to 154.

After the Commons vote, Palmerston decided to bring matters to a head. He warned the Brazilian chargé in London that Britain was prepared to take even harsher measures to end the slave trade and threatened to occupy part of the Brazilian coast. In April the Foreign Office advised the admiralty that, with the demise of the 1817 treaty, Britain was no longer legally obligated to respect Brazilian territorial waters and ports. Britain had already violated Brazil's territorial waters on numerous occasions, but Palmerston's urgings and the newly discovered legal justification led to bolder action. On June 22 the local British admiral ordered his ships to enter Brazilian ports as well as territorial waters in pursuit of slavers. The next day two British boats seized a slaver in the port of Macae, pulling it away under fire from the guns in the harbor. A week later a different British warship towed three slavers from the port of Panagua, burning two of them within sight of the harbor's fort.

The Brazilian Council of State, angered and intimidated, met on 11 July 1850 to discuss the British actions. Historian Leslie Bethell describes these meetings:

> despite a good deal of fighting talk . . . it seemed . . . clear that Brazil was virtually powerless to resist the British navy and that any attempt to do so could only aggravate the situation: Brazilian commerce would be completely paralyzed with serious consequences for the entire Brazilian economy and for public revenue, the slave population might be dangerously inflamed, the recently established internal stability would be threatened and, always a most important consideration, Brazil's position would be seriously weakened in the coming confrontation with [Argentine dictator] Rosas in the Rio de la Plata if she were at the same time involved in a conflict with Britain. Moreover, since to resist British pressure would be tantamount to an open defence of the slave trade, Brazil could expect no outside support in her hour of need.[23]

In fact, Brazil approached the French minister for aid, but he "made it absolutely clear that on this issue Brazil stood alone." Unlike many of today's human rights violators, Brazil could find no refuge in great-power rivalry. Two days later the foreign minister, Paulino Soares de Sousa, met with the British envoy and promised to take effective measures against the slave trade. In return he asked for and received a promise that the seizures of slavers in ports would stop, at least temporarily. On July 15, Paulino, a conservative who represented a slave-owning area, explained to the Brazilian Chamber why the government intended at last to stop the slave trade. Paulino, writes Bethell, "made no attempt to disguise the fact that it was British pressure that had finally compelled Brazil to end the slave trade—he said little about the growth of Brazilian abolitionism."[24]

In fact, 1849 and 1850 had seen a small growth in Brazilian support for abolition of the slave trade, due in large measure to fears of "Africanization" caused by the massive influx of slaves from 1846 to 1849. This change of heart was, however, limited to a small urban elite. Similar fears had waxed and waned following the large slave imports of 1827 to 1830 and after a slave revolt in Bahia in 1835. Brazil, Paulino told the Chamber,

> is now the only nation which had not acquiesced in this [anti–slave-trade] system. . . . The greater the facilities are for covering these speculations with our flag the greater will be the number of insults which we shall have daily to suffer. . . It is natural that England should on each occasion press us more and more. . . . Can we resist the torrent? I think not.[25]

The Brazilian government immediately sent out orders to the provinces for the suppression of the slave trade. Local officials were ordered to demolish the barracks for holding newly landed slaves and to prevent ships from fitting out for the trade. It was made clear that the orders had to be followed. Most of the slave traders were Portuguese, and the government attempted to take advantage of latent anti-Portuguese feeling. A number of slave traders were deported. The Chamber of Deputies passed a tough law against the slave trade in September 1850, and Brazil herself established a naval patrol against the slave trade.

Palmerston, however, remained distrustful of Brazilian intentions and demanded that the British navy be allowed to patrol the waters and ports of Brazil in company with the Brazilian navy. Paulino refused, claiming that, despite a few landings in Bahia, Brazil was ending the slave trade rapidly. The British envoy in Brazil acted in accordance with Palmerston's instructions and on 11 January 1851 informed Paulino that the British fleet would resume its actions of the previous summer. The effect of this message, the envoy reported, was "magical and ludicrous."[26] The next day the government sent every available Brazilian steamship, a party of armed police on board, on patrol against the slave trade. In the following months the slave trade was finally crushed. The clear signs of this were a near doubling of prices for slaves in Brazil and a collapse of prices in Africa.

The Role of British Force

Leslie Bethell, the most careful historian of these events, draws the following conclusion about what ended the slave trade to Brazil:

> Both sides . . . claimed the credit for having suppressed the trade. And, in so doing, both exaggerated the extent of their own responsibility. . . . The trade was finally and completely crushed . . . largely, though not entirely, because for the very first time a Brazilian government decided to take effective action against it and, more important, had the authority and the

resources to implement this decision. There is evidence to show that for a variety of reasons (which included the reappearance of a British preventive squadron in Brazilian territorial waters and the deteriorating situation in the Rio de la Plata, as well as purely domestic political considerations) the Brazilian government had for some time been cautiously considering what steps could be taken to put down the trade. And, as they later claimed, legislation had actually been drafted before the middle of 1850. *It is clear, however, that it was the sudden extension in June and July of the British squadron's anti-slave trade operations into Brazilian inland waters and ports which,* by provoking a major political crisis in Brazil, *led directly to the passage of a new anti-slave trade law and to its vigorous enforcement.* It is fruitless to speculate when, or even whether, such a law would have been passed—much less enforced—had Britain not intervened decisively at this critical juncture. At the very least, British naval action could be said to have greatly accelerated, if it did not alone precipitate, Brazil's own, ultimately successful, efforts to suppress the slave trade.[27]

For the British ministers most closely involved, the reason for the end of the slave trade was simple: British force. Typical was the comment of the British envoy in Brazil in 1840. No Brazilian government, he wrote, could be trusted to cooperate willingly in the suppression of the slave trade.

The employment or perhaps the mere display of force on our part is, I am sorry to say, the only efficacious mode of enabling the well disposed part of the administration to outweigh their opponents . . . on this question; of course, the naval force is that to which I allude.[28]

Some comtemporary Brazilian leaders claimed that the end of the slave trade came as a result of "revolution in [Brazilian] public opinion."[29] This assertion has been repeated more recently by a number of historians. Palmerston, who directed British policy, completely rejected this interpretation of events. The end of the slave trade to Brazil "is proof of the eminent success of our naval operations. Tell me that it is the result of improved opinion in Brazil! I treat that assertion with the contempt that it deserves. No man who knows anything of Brazil or the facts of the case will entertain such a position for a moment."[30] In keeping with his view that only force or the threat of force could bring Brazil to cooperate in ending the slave trade, Palmerston refused repeated requests from the Brazilian government to repeal the Aberdeen Act, which the Brazilians considered an affront to national dignity.

The bill of 1845 is the only security against the revival of the Brazilian slave trade and *it ought never to be repealed.* The sincerity of the Brazilian government against the slave trade is the sincerity with which a pickpocket keeps his hands from a bystander's coat flaps while he sees a policeman's eye fixed upon him.[31]

Palmerston's view prevailed throughout his lifetime. He died in 1865; Parliament waited until 1869 to repeal the Aberdeen Act.

The slave trade ended quickly after Britain adopted much more forceful tactics against Brazil. This raises the question whether the policy of mutual search treaties and naval patrols was a mistaken approach. As we noted earlier, the campaign against the slave trade did take a long time.

Despite the efforts of the West African squadron, an estimated 560,000 slaves entered Brazil between 1830 and 1850. The commander-in-chief of the West African squadron from October 1846 to March 1849 termed the anti–slave-trade measures in force during that period, the most active in the squadron's existence, "perfectly futile."[32] For the campaign to succeed, he believed, Brazil had to be persuaded to cooperate—by war if necessary. Palmerston's opposition to the withdrawal of the squadron did not imply a lack of recognition of the squadron's inability to end the slave trade on its own. He had long believed that the squadron should be strengthened and an additional contingent placed off Brazil. From 1847 he seriously considered the possibility of a blockade of Brazilian harbors as a means of forcing Brazil to cooperate: "Our navy wants exercise and practice in time of peace, and Rio would do . . . well for that purpose."[33] The commander-in-chief of the West African squadron quoted above exaggerated, however, when he called the patrol's work completely futile. The squadron certainly succeeded in reducing the slave trade, even if it could not eliminate it. It freed about 8 percent of the number of slaves estimated to have been successfully carried across and, especially in the later period, seized numerous ships equipped for the slave trade though not carrying slaves. This harassment led to a rise in the price of slaves in Brazil, which, as might be expected, caused a drop in the demand for slaves in areas where they were economically marginal. Speaking of the period before 1850, one historian writes:

> The ban on the traffic was effective . . . in the extreme southern provinces and on the long northern coast between Cape Sao Roque and the Amazon . . . this partial cessation of the slave trade was not the result of conscientious officials or a law-abiding population. Rather, it occurred because of the higher cost of slaves brought on by the British policing efforts.[34]

Moreover, it would be wrong to see the number of captures and their economic effect as the only measure of the squadron's effectiveness. It served as a highly visible symbol of a great power's real commitment to pursue its human rights policy. Reliance on the British navy to end the slave trade also had the virtue of reducing the risk of war, because it required minimal Brazilian participation; as it happened, however, Britain did not have to go to war to persuade Brazil to take effective action against the slave trade.

The Preconditions of British Success

Could Britain have ended the slave trade twenty years earlier by employing in 1830 the strong tactics used in 1850? Bethell, the most thorough student of the problem, implies that Britain would have had more difficulty in obtaining Brazilian cooperation. "In 1850, Brazil had for the first time a government with sufficient authority and power to enforce its will."[35] Brazil experienced numerous provincial revolts between 1830 and 1849. Had the central government attempted to enforce abolition of the slave trade earlier than 1850, Bethell seems to imply, it might have caused an insurrection and, possibly, the breakup of the country. On the other hand, since Brazilian slaveholders produced largely for foreign markets, they were directly vulnerable to British blockade. The British envoy in Brazil reported in 1848 that both Bahia and Rio de Janeiro could be effectively blockaded—"no port in the world is capable of being so easily blockaded than [sic] Rio."[36] If Britain had applied a blockade, it is difficult to see how Brazilian slaveholders, facing economic ruin, could have resisted for long.

It would appear that the later tactics were more effective than the search treaty and naval patrol approach. But the two approaches should not be seen as mutually exclusive. The years of naval patroling under the mutual search treaties established the legitimacy of taking steps against the slave trade and thus of the more drastic measures Britain eventually took. In this way the earlier precedent undoubtedly diminished the price Britain would have had to pay for any sudden infringement of Brazil's sovereignty.

We are now in a position to sum up the preconditions for the elimination of the slave trade to Brazil. The national interest of Brazil would not have ended this traffic for a long time. To end it required an active human rights policy pursued by a great power, Britain. The enormous military strength of Britain was an essential factor. So was its willingness to use this power; the interventionism or bellicosity of Palmerston had to dominate over the British impulses toward pacifism and toward recognition of the right of Brazil to determine its own destiny. Finally, although the abolition of the Atlantic slave trade was essentially achieved by British action, that action was immensely assisted by an international consensus against the trade. As we have seen, Brazilian officials could feel that Brazil was the only nation standing against a "torrent" of international opinion. Because of the Victorian consensus of all "civilized" nations against the slave trade, Brazilian appeals to other powers such as France were in vain. The other major powers, however much they may have been rivals of Britain, generally regarded it as improper to exploit against Britain the indignation aroused by the human rights campaign.

In this last respect we are very distant from nineteenth-century conditions. When the United States curtailed aid to Ethiopia as a response to the terror that followed the Ethiopian revolution, the Soviet Union exploited this opening to supplant the United States in Ethiopia. It is not only the Soviet Union that behaves in this way. A number of nations have made use of the repugnance felt against the methods of the PLO (Palestine Liberation Organization) to get close to that organization for their own purposes. The United States has not always disdained this course. When the Khmer Rouge regime in Cambodia collapsed under the weight of its own infamies, the U.S. attitude toward continued diplomatic recognition of that regime was not determined by its general condemnation of their crimes; we saw the occasion as an opportunity to demonstrate our usefulness to China and our opposition to Viet Nam.

The State Department's *Country Reports* have asserted for a number of years that "there now exists an international consensus that recognizes basic human rights and obligations owed by all governments to their citizens." Sometimes it is even suggested that consensus is growing: "The year 1979 saw impressive strides . . . in building regional and international institutions for the protection of basic human rights [reflecting] growing recognition that human rights abuses are a legitimate subject of concern."[37] Such a view covers over the tragic facts and prevents us from dealing with one of the greatest problems facing a serious human rights policy.

The stern measures taken by Britain against Brazil raise a continuing issue in human rights policy: Does it necessarily involve the sacrifice of the national interest? Britain did earn the animosity of most Brazilians by her unrelenting pressure on the slave trade. But she seems to have paid very little, in tangible terms, for incurring Brazilian disfavor. True, Brazilian anger over the Aberdeen Act prevented the renewal of the commercial treaty granting Britain a privileged economic position when that treaty expired in 1844, but Britain's economic superiority over its rivals prevented any perceptible economic losses. "The historic privileges enjoyed by England in Portuguese possessions for centuries ceased to exist in Brazil without damage to British trade," concludes Alan Manchester.[38] In fact, British exports to Brazil almost doubled in the 1850s, jumping from £2,545,000 in 1850 to £4,447,000 in 1860. Manchester does argue, however, that as a result of bitterness stemming from the slave-trade struggle, Brazil became politically estranged from Britain and more closely allied with the United States:

> England's attempt to abolish the slave traffic was the direct cause of the decline of its political preeminence in Portuguese America. From the very moment of the signature of the convention in 1826 until the late 'sixties, Anglo-Brazilian relations were embittered by the slave trade, the distrust and contempt of the British (for the Brazilians) being matched by the fear and hatred of the Brazilians in whose mind the suppression of the traffic and subordination to England were synonymous.[39]

In 1863 two relatively minor incidents—the murder of ten British seamen shipwrecked in a remote part of Brazil and the accidental jailing of several British sailors on leave in Rio de Janeiro—found Brazil and Britain still so distrustful of each other that diplomatic relations were briefly broken off. Manchester does not indicate, however, whether Britain's political decline in Brazil ever led to any tangible disadvantages. Britain's economic preeminence in Brazil was seriously challenged for the first time at the end of the nineteenth century, and only in 1924 did U.S. exports to Brazil overtake British exports. It was the excellence of U.S. and German goods, British consuls reported in the late nineteenth century, that led to their success in competition with British products.

The Slave Trade From Zanzibar to Arabia

The second major area of the slave trade originated in the African borderlands of the Muslim world in West Africa, the southern Sudan, and East Africa.[40] The slaves were caught in raids on pagan communities and traded north to Arabia, the Ottoman Empire, and Egypt. The most important routes of the Muslim slave trade extended up the Nile from the Egyptian Sudan and from the island of Zanzibar by sea to Arabia. The Egyptian government, acting partly under Western pressure and partly in response to the attractiveness of the European example, gradually reduced slaving and the slave trade within the Egyptian empire; these were ended by the British occupation of the Sudan in 1898. Here we will follow the story of the other major route, from East Africa to Arabia by way of Zanzibar.

Zanzibar became a center for the slave trade to Arabia at the end of the seventeenth century, when the Arab rulers of Oman took the island from Portugal. Slaves were captured far inland and taken in convoys to the cities along the coast, which, from Cape Delgado in the south to the Benadir parts of Somalia, was nominally part of the domain of the sultan of Zanzibar. From the coast the slaves were shipped to Zanzibar. Arab slave traders, chiefly from the Persian Gulf, arrived in Zanzibar in winter, using the northeast monsoon, and took their cargoes away by dhow in the spring, when the winds changed direction. Although the dominance of Zanzibar was new, the slave trade from East Africa to Arabia was ancient. It had begun by the eighth century, when Arab traders began settling on the coast of East Africa, or earlier. The scale of this traffic during the nineteenth century was substantial, although precise figures are hard to obtain. A British captain who visited Zanzibar in 1811 estimated that between 6,000 and 10,000 slaves were shipped annually from the island to the Middle East. Sixty years later a British parliamentary committee studying the East African slave trade estimated that from 1867 to 1869 Arab slave traders took 37,000 slaves from Zanzibar and the opposite coast. Many of the slaves sold on Zanzibar remained on the island and worked the clove plantations; in 1860 approximately two-thirds of the estimated 300,000 people on Zanzibar were slaves.

In the nineteenth century this ancient commerce was destined to confront the conception of decency held by Victorian Britain. Great Britain was the dominant European power on the coast of East Africa. Portugal had long been in decline; its control of Mozambique was tenuous, and it was in no position to threaten other areas. France had lost Mauritius, the Seychelles, and most of its Indian possessions in the wars of the late eighteenth and early nineteenth centuries; with these colonies went much of French influence in the Indian Ocean. France retained the island of Réunion and several trading posts on Madagascar, however, and from these bases succeeded in creating various troubles for Britain. For example, France continued the slave trade to Réunion, thinly disguised as "free contract labor," into the second half of the nineteenth century, and occasionally intrigued in the political struggles in Zanzibar, though with no lasting damage to British interests. In 1862 France signed an agreement with Britain in which both powers promised to respect the sovereignty of Zanzibar. This treaty, by committing France to the status quo, confirmed Britain's political and military preeminence in East Africa. Only in 1885, when Germany suddenly claimed a large portion of East Africa as a colony, was British preeminence seriously challenged.

Until the arrival of Germany, the sultanate of Zanzibar was the major state in East Africa, and Britain achieved its goals in the area—preventing other powers from seizing bases there, protecting British capital and lives and those of the numerous British Indian subjects living in Zanzibar, and abolishing the slave trade—through its influence on Zanzibar. Zanzibar's economy was based on the sea trade in cloves, ivory, and slaves, and this made the country particularly vulnerable to British seapower. Moreover, Indians who had settled in East Africa financed much of Zanzibar's trade, and Britain and British India together were Zanzibar's largest non-Arab trading partner for much of the nineteenth century. British influence was shown by the role it played in determining the succession to the sultanate on the death of Saiyid Said, the sultan of Zanzibar and Oman from 1806 to 1856. Said had appointed one son, Majid, ruler of Zanzibar, and a second, Thuwaini, ruler of Oman. Thuwaini was not content with the division because the revenues of Zanzibar far exceeded those of Oman, and in 1859 he sent a fleet to take Zanzibar for himself. The British governor of Bombay decided to prevent the impending war off East Africa and halted Thuwaini's fleet by dispatching several warships to the mouth of the Persian Gulf. Britain offered to arbitrate the dispute, and Thuwaini felt obliged to accept the offer. Britain's envoys confirmed the division of the kingdom but awarded Oman a portion of Zanzibar's revenues to make up for the disparity in the resources of the two countries. Britain also acted to preserve Majid's rule against the intrigues of a third brother, Barghash, who lived on Zanzibar and revolted after the failure of Thuwaini's invasion became known. Barghash was arrested by British troops and sent to

Bombay for a year. On Majid's death in 1870 Barghash became sultan, with British acquiescence.

The market for most of the slaves shipped north from Zanzibar was the Persian Gulf region. This area was also dominated by Britain throughout the nineteenth century. Britain had extended its influence among the tribes and countries of the Gulf to protect the flank of India and British commerce and lives. British India's trade with the Gulf rose from approximately £800,000 in 1836–37 to £4,045,000 in 1877–78. Britain fought piracy and tried, with mixed success, to restrain the incessant warring of local Arab tribes. In the winter of 1819–20, for example, eleven warships of the British navy and the East India Company, together with 3,500 British and Indian troops, captured a pirate center on the Trucial Coast and secured a promise that the raids would stop.

On the north shore of the Gulf, relations with Persia were troubled. Despite an 1814 treaty that promised Persia British aid in the event of an attack by a European power, Britain declined to intervene in the Russo-Persian war of 1826–28. Persia lost the war, and Britain lost influence to Russia. Twice, in 1838 and again in 1856, Persia attacked Afghanistan on Russian urging; Britain wanted to preserve Afghanistan as a buffer for India. On both occasions Britain occupied Persian territory in the Gulf in retaliation, forcing Persia to pull back from Afghanistan. Turkey, the other major state bordering on the Persian Gulf, relied on Britain for protection against enemies such as Mehemet Ali, pasha of Egypt, as well as Russia, and was therefore highly vulnerable to British pressure on the slave trade.

Confronting Local Opposition

The British campaign to abolish the slave trade had no local support in East Africa and the Persian Gulf. A whole network of slave traders and owners relied on the slave trade for their livelihoods. Slavery and the slave trade had the sanction of Islamic law. The sultan of Zanzibar levied a tax on each slave shipped north, and this revenue constituted one of his chief sources of income. In attempting to suppress the slave trade in the face of popular sentiment, Britain always faced the danger of provoking resistance that would have imperiled its other objectives in the area: stability, protection of British lives and commerce, the growth of British influence. Moreover, Britain wanted to avoid having to commit large numbers of ships or troops to East Africa or the Persian Gulf, and the suppression of revolts undoubtedly would have involved force or the show of force. On the other hand, if Britain was not willing to risk antagonizing the local population, it could not hope to abolish the slave trade. This tension between the possible consequences of Britain's campaign against the slave trade and Britain's other goals in East Africa and the Persian Gulf helped determine the pace of the campaign and the tactics used. As it happened, Britain succeeded in ending the slave trade from Zanzibar without seriously compromising its other interests in the area.

Between 1820 and 1845 Britain made several efforts to persuade Saiyid Said, sultan of Zanzibar and Oman, to ban the slave trade to his subjects. When first approached in 1821, Said rejected the appeal, declaring that the reasons were "clear . . . as the Moon and the Sun."[41] In the following year, however, he agreed to prohibit the sale of slaves to Christians (this clause was aimed at the smuggling of slaves to Mauritius and the French island of Réunion) and to British India. In return he received, in addition to the vague benefits of British favor, reduced customs rates on trade to Mauritius. Two years later, Said suffered one of the perils of defying British popular opinion on the slave trade. A British captain, acting on his own initiative, occupied the coastal city of Mombasa, nominally a part of Said's empire but at the beginning of 1824 in revolt. He remained there for two years and used his position as a means of pressuring the sultan to abolish the slave trade. Said actually agreed to do so but demanded in return monetary compensation, Portuguese Mozambique, or a British promise to defend both parts of his country, on land and sea. These demands Britain refused to grant, and in 1826 the British government ended this peculiar episode by ordering British troops withdrawn from Mombasa. The Court of Directors of the East India Company gave the rationale for this decision the following year in its instructions to its agent in Bombay. Sultan Said, the court wrote, had already made

> as great a concession as could possibly have been expected from a prince in his circumstances. . . . It is essential . . . that nothing should be done to diminish his authority and influence as a Mahometan Prince, especially as it is contrary to our policy, and altogether foreign from our purpose, to interfere for his defence against the people of Arabia, which nevertheless we should be bound in common justice to do if his safety were to be actually endangered by measures which we should have forced on him after the strong assurances he has made, and the reasons he has given to show that it would be so endangered. . . . For these reasons we must recommend to you to press the Imam no further on this point.[42]

In 1841, after Britain's success in forcing Mehemet Ali back to Egypt, Lord Palmerston, then foreign secretary, proposed that Said again be pressured to end the slave trade. In a letter shown to Said in January 1841, the Foreign Office held that "so strong a feeling against the Slave Trade and so deep a sense of its criminality have grown up in the minds of the English nation that the British government cannot avoid using its utmost means to prevent the continuance of such proceedings wherever it may be able to do so."[43] The letter went on to claim, falsely, that existing treaties gave Britain the right to suppress the slave trade unilaterally and Britain threatened to act on this right. This effort to force the abolition of the slave trade from Zanzibar by using threats aroused the opposition of the governor-general of India. In February 1842 he wrote to the Foreign Office that Britain

> must trust to time and favourable circumstances for the accomplishment of its humane views, rather than to a course of violent and arbitrary proceedings which would unite against us the interests, habits, and feelings of all the states and communities along the shores of the Gulf. Other powers are ready to take advantage of the prejudice against us which the belief of our resolution everywhere to suppress slavery is calculated to excite among the tribes of eastern Africa and Arabia. . . . His Lordship in Council cannot but think that the delay of a few years in the final extinction of this traffic is far less evil than the annihilation of that political influence by which the British government may fairly hope to effect so much for the cause of humanity.[44]

Just as today, the fear of giving rival powers an advantage in the countries criticized for human rights violations acted as a deterrent to pursuing a policy on behalf of human rights.

Lord Aberdeen, who succeeded Palmerston as foreign secretary in November 1841, persisted in pressing Said for an immediate end to the slave trade, though he did not act on Palmerston's threats. In 1845 Said agreed to ban the slave trade from Zanzibar to Arabia and gave the ships of Britain and the East India Company the right to search dhows for slaves. The treaty did not, however, prohibit the slave trade between the coast of Africa and Zanzibar. The sultan had made an enormous concession to Britain. J. B. Kelly, the historian of British relations with the Gulf states, expresses some puzzlement at Said's willingness to sign the 1845 treaty. Perhaps, he suggests, Said's age had led him to care less about the responsibility of governing.[45] Moreover, Sultan Said had been under the impression when he signed the treaty that Zanzibar would receive some financial compensation from Britain as part of the bargain. Palmerston had offered Said £6,000 in 1841, and Lord Aberdeen had given a verbal assurance that some sort of payment would be made. The treaty itself did not mention compensation, however, and when Palmerston returned to the Foreign Office in 1846 he refused to give Said anything. His note to the British envoy in Zanzibar conveys the spirit in which Palmerston conducted negotiations on the slave trade with non-European countries.

> Captain Hamerton should take every opportunity of impressing upon these Arabs that the nations of Europe are destined to put an end to the African S.T., and that Great Britain is the main instrument in the Hands of Providence for the accomplishment of this purpose. That it is in vain for these Arabs to endeavour to resist the consummation of that which is written in the Book of Fate, and that they ought to bow to superior power, to leave off a pursuit which is doomed to annihilation, and a perseverance in which will only involve them in losses and other evils;

and that they should hasten to betake themselves to the cultivation of their soil and to lawful and innocent commerce.[46]

This passage is striking for a number of reasons. First, it is remarkable that Palmerston could speak of the still flourishing slave trade as "a pursuit doomed to annihilation." The slave trade had not even been abolished in Britain itself forty years earlier, but Palmerston speaks of its abolition as a "consummation . . . written in the Book of Fate." Palmerston's instructions to Hamerton convey an unshakable assurance that British power would be irresistible and that Britain was unquestionably in the right: Britain is the "main instrument in the Hands of Providence." It is clear that Britain came to its human rights campaign against the slave trade with the attitude of self-confidence that we know to have characterized the Victorian age in general. In foreign policy as well as other areas, the Victorians were sure that they were guided by the right purposes and that the victory of these purposes was assured by their own abilities and by the force of progress. In the years following World War I the self-confidence of the Victorians has been extensively criticized, and there is no doubt that it frequently degenerated into an insufferable complacency about themselves and an arrogance toward other societies. But, however one might object to this nineteenth-century self-confidence simply as an expression of the human spirit, its consequences for the campaign against the slave trade were surely the ones we would want. It appears to have been one of the preconditions for the success of that campaign.

Sultan Said had agreed to the abolition of the slave trade from Zanzibar, but he had neither the means nor the will to enforce his undertaking. The two or three British ships available for anti–slave-trade patrol could only harass the traffic. But the 1845 treaty did cause a temporary decline in the slave trade from Zanzibar. "There is certainly not one-fifth part of the Slave Trade carried on from the Imam's [sic] African dominions which used to be a few years ago," reported the British envoy in Zanzibar in 1850.[47] The reduction in the number of slaves exported from Zanzibar was in part made up for, however, by an increase in the number of slaves imported into the Persian Gulf from Abyssinia.

The Impact of British Pressure

Having obtained a treaty from Zanzibar, Britain turned its attention to the markets for the slave trade in the Persian Gulf. The first country to succumb to British pressure was Turkey. Turkey had first been approached on the matter of curtailing the slave trade throughout its empire in 1840. That suggestion, the British ambassador reported, had been "heard with extreme astonishment accompanied with a smile."[48] Turkey was not substantially involved in the slave trade in the Persian Gulf and offered little resistance when the British chargé d'affaires proposed in 1846 that Turkey prohibit its citizens from engaging in the East African slave trade. The following year the sultan issued a firman to that effect and gave Britain the right to search and seize Turkish ships suspected of slaving. The desire for British favor also appears to have sufficed to convince six of the smaller Arab principalities of the Gulf to follow Turkey's example. The sheikhs of Qawasim, 'Ajman, Dubai, Umm Al-Qaiwain, Abu Dhabi, and Bahrain all signed treaties with Britain banning the slave trade to their subjects and giving Britain the rights of search and seizure.

Persia proved less accommodating. In the course of trying to overcome the shah's religious scruples about ending the slave trade, the British envoy went so far as to obtain opinions denouncing the trade from several Muslim clerics. Finally, in July 1847, after a year of negotiations, Palmerston ordered the British envoy in Teheran to inform the shah that Britain was prepared to seize all slave ships it found in the Persian Gulf, with or without a treaty. In June 1848 the shah banned the East African slave trade to Persia. J. B. Kelly, it should be noted, declines to attribute the shah's change of heart to Palmerston's ultimatum and suggests that the settling of certain border disputes between Turkey and Persia, in which Britain had played a part, may have had something to do with the Persian decision.[49] The shah refused, however, to give Britain the right to search Persian ships. He feared that such a concession might lead to comparable encroachments on Persia's sovereignty by Russia, whose actions had indicated that she was willing to use such excuses. The shah also feared that such visible subservience to Britain might lower Persian prestige among the tribes then loyal to Persia. In May 1850, after two years of negotiation on this point, Palmerston ordered the British navy to begin searching Persian ships despite the absence of a treaty. In November a treaty still was not forthcoming, and Palmerston gave the screw one more turn. "When next the Persian Minister asks the good offices or interference of England on behalf of Persia, in any matter whatever," he wrote the British envoy in Teheran, "you should say that you much regret that you are precluded by your instructions from complying with that request."[50] The following year Persia compromised; it allowed British ships to search and seize Persian vessels but demanded that a Persian officer be on board the British ship to supervise. In 1882 Persia granted Britain the right to search without Persian supervision. It is clear that, as in the case of the Atlantic slave trade, British willingness to act unilaterally and often in defiance of the equality of states was a major factor in what Britain achieved.

Britain expended a great deal of diplomatic energy obtaining anti–slave-trade treaties, but through the 1850s and 1860s there were not nearly enough cruisers to make their provisions effective. In 1852 only two ships were placed on anti–slave-trade patrol in the Gulf, in 1853 one and in 1854 again one. The death of Saiyid Said in 1856 weakened the authority of the government of Zanzibar, with the result that the slave trade from Zanzibar revived. Slave traders from the Persian Gulf openly defied Sultan Majid, and during their stay in Zanzibar they looted, brawled, and kidnapped. By the early 1860s the slave trade from Zanzibar was as large as it had ever been. "I believe that not even one percent of the slaves taken north every year are captured by British cruisers," commented the British envoy in Zanzibar in 1867.[51]

In the late 1860s and early 1870s Britain renewed its attack on the East African slave trade, concentrating on stopping it at its source, Zanzibar. Among the reasons for the revival of British efforts—in addition to the obvious inadequacy of the steps taken earlier—was the publication, beginning in 1857, of David Livingstone's accounts of his travels in Africa, with detailed and gruesome descriptions of the consequences of the slave trade. "The many skeletons we have seen, amongst the rocks and woods, by the little ponds and along the paths of wilderness, attest the awful sacrifice of human life, which must be attributed, directly or indirectly, to this trade of hell," wrote Livingstone in a book published in 1865.[52] Elsewhere he wrote, "No one can estimate the amount of good that will be done if this awful Slave Trade be abolished. This will be something to have lived for."[53] Livingstone's revelations aroused public interest in East Africa and in the slave trade. In July 1871 the government appointed a parliamentary committee to investigate the state of the slave trade off East Africa. It concluded that the sultan of Zanzibar should be persuaded to take more active measures. In particular, the committee decided that the sultan should end the slave trade from the coast of Africa to the island of Zanzibar. "Any attempt to supply slaves for domestic use in Zanzibar will always be a pretext and cloak for a foreign trade."[54] The following year a mission headed by Sir Bartle Frere left for Zanzibar to accomplish the aims set out by the committee.

The British had to deal with a new sultan, Barghash, Majid having died in 1870. As a means of inducing the British envoy to support his ascension to the throne, Barghash had promised his support for a tougher treaty against the slave trade, but once in power he promptly disowned this pledge. It is an indication of how seriously Britain took the anti–slave-trade campaign that, on learning of Barghash's change of mind, the British envoy immediately notified his superiors of "how desirable it would be to unseat him [Barghash] on the first pretext."[55] Barghash was aware of this hostility, for he secretly appealed to Germany (which had just defeated France) for protection against Britain. Bismarck was not interested, and Barghash learned to be somewhat more flexible in his dealings with the British. The latter, in turn, learned to live with Barghash; no attempts were made to dethrone him. Sultan Barghash's relations with Britain were still somewhat cool when Sir Bartle Frere arrived in Zanzibar in 1873. Barghash heard Frere out, but after consulting with his advisors he refused to sign the treaty. The sultan's decision owed something to intrigue by the French consul, who hinted that if Barghash resisted the British, France might provide support.

Having failed to obtain a treaty, Frere, on leaving Zanzibar, issued instructions to the British navy to stop the slave trade between Zanzibar island and the coast. As this coast was also part of the sultanate of Zanzibar, and the boats used often flew its flag, this action constituted flagrant interference in the internal affairs of another state. For a month two British warships effectively ended the slave trade to Zanzibar. "From Kilwa [the major slave trading center on the coast] not a single slave has yet escaped and the Arab owners, driven to desperation, are selling off the strongest ones at very reduced prices to speculators who propose attempting their transport by land," reported the British consul in Zanzibar, John Kirk.[56] At the end of the month Kirk, on instructions from London, informed Barghash that if he did not sign a treaty banning the slave trade, the British navy would seal off Zanzibar to trade of all kinds. "I have not come to discuss," he told Barghash, "but to dictate."[57] Sultan Barghash had in the meantime discovered that the French envoy had exceeded his instructions in promising to protect Zanzibar from Britain. Two days after Kirk delivered his ultimatum, Barghash signed the treaty. The agreement committed Barghash to fight the seagoing slave trade "to the best of his ability," and to shut the slave market in Zanzibar.

The Extinction of the Zanzibar Slave Trade

The new cooperation of the sultan of Zanzibar with the British was not completely unrequited. Ever since he came to power, Barghash had refused to pay the annual subsidy to Oman, which Britain had awarded to that country in 1860 as a means of preserving the peace. In return for Barghash's decision to sign the anti–slave-trade treaty Britain agreed to make the payment, about £8,000 per year. The government of India paid the subsidy until 1947, at which point Britain assumed the obligation. At least through 1968 Britain continued to make the payment.

Once Britain had made clear the price of resistance, Barghash co-operated fully. Not only did he stop the slave trade to Zanzibar, but when slave traders began smuggling slaves to the neighboring island of Pemba on a large scale and evading the ban on shipping slaves by marching them up the coast in convoys, he took effective countermeasures. In 1876 Barghash issued a proclamation banning the inland slave trade. To aid in the enforcement of this edict the sultan took an astonishing step for a still-traditional Muslim society. He decreed the abolition of slavery itself in several towns in the northern part of his domains. The 1876 proclamation produced major rebellions in the coastal cities of Kilwa and Mombasa, but with the aid of the British navy (in the case of Kilwa) the sultan reestablished his authority. When Barghash discovered in 1877 that the governor of Kilwa, a relative, was personally involved in the slave trade, he had him jailed. "It is now understood that slave dealing is an offence not to be passed over because of rank or family influence," reported Kirk.[58]

By 1880 large-scale slave trading from Zanzibar and the opposite coast had ended. Small-time smuggling continued for many years, however, and a local famine and the instability caused by the scramble for Africa led to a temporary revival of the slave trade in the mid 1880s. The last slave dhow seized off East Africa was taken in 1899. In Zanzibar itself the abolition of slavery followed the ending of the slave trade. In 1890, the year Britain made Zanzibar a protectorate, Barghash's successor forbade the exchange, sale, or purchase of slaves within Zanzibar. In 1896 Britain intervened in a succession struggle in Zanzibar and succeeded, through a naval bombardment, in defeating the forces of a contender known to be anti-British. Britain pressed the new sultan on the slavery issue, and in 1897 he abolished the legal status of slavery on Zanzibar and Pemba; ten years later he declared slavery illegal on the mainland. The practical effect was that courts would no longer enforce slaveowner's rights against slaves. Parliament allocated a small sum of money to compensate slaveowners, and from 1897 to 1907 this fund paid out £8,125. In 1909 the sultan issued a decree banning slavery altogether.

The power of Great Britain, and her willingness to use it, provided a solid structure of rewards for Barghash's cooperation. A number of incidents showed him how valuable it was to be in Britain's good graces. In January 1875 the garrison of Mombasa rebelled against the sultan and barricaded themselves in the fort. The British envoy in Zanzibar promptly dispatched a warship to Mombasa. A two-and-one-half-hour bombardment by the British ship ended the revolt. Later that same year a small Egyptian fleet seized several towns in Somalia that had traditionally been included in Barghash's dominions. At this time France and Britain in large measure dominated the Egyptian government, and when Kirk protested to London about the incursion, the Egyptian forces were immediately withdrawn. In 1877 Kirk decided that Zanzibar needed a better army, partly in order to prevent the flouting of Sultan Barghash's decrees on the slave trade. Kirk persuaded a British lieutenant to head and train the force, and in 1878 the British government presented the army with 500 rifles and ammunition. The Foreign Office note stated that this gift was to show British appreciation for "the loyalty and good faith with which His Highness has carried out his treaty engagements with this country for the suppression of the Slave Trade in his domains."[59] The British campaign to end the East African slave trade could never have succeeded in overcoming the traditional structure of Zanzibari society and the interests of so many of the sultan's subjects in the absence of the enormous power and influence Britain possessed in that area.

It is a remarkable paradox that British influence in Zanzibar and the authority of the sultanate both rose dramatically after Britain forced Barghash to abolish the slave trade. One reason for this was that, despite the predictions of ruin made by some Arabs, other commerce soon took the place of the slave trade. In 1880 Kirk's assistant made the following report on the condition of what formerly had been the largest slave-trading city on the coast:

> India-rubber is now the principal export, though cereals and sesamum seed bid fair to rival it in importance, and the trade in coral is reviving quickly. . . . Everywhere in the Indian quarters substantial stone buildings are replacing the old mud and stub shops and houses. . . . The improvement in the attitude of the people is equally marked. In fact, both British and Arab subjects have at last become convinced, through the all-powerful logic of a full pocket, that, after all, Great Britain was furthering their real interests in insisting on the total suppression of the Slave Trade.[60]

It was clear to everyone that Barghash had yielded to superior force, and this shielded him. Kirk wrote later that he believed the sultan would have been killed had he signed the 1873 treaty when it was first broached. But since he had waited until Britain forced his hand, Kirk thought that Barghash's attack on the slave trade had actually increased his authority. Relations between Barghash and Kirk were so close that Kirk became, as Sir Reginald Coupland put it, "a sort of unofficial prime minister of Zanzibar."[61] In the later years of his rule Barghash showed Kirk all his correspondence with foreign countries and relied heavily on Kirk's advice. In 1881 Barghash went so far as to ask Britain to serve as the guardian of the sultanate after he died and before his sons came of age.

The conclusion seems to be that the national interest of Great Britain did not suffer very seriously because of the locally unpopular campaign against the East African slave trade. We can provisionally identify the following reasons for this. First, Britain had enormous power relative to the communities that sold slaves and bought them. Second, this power took the form of sea power, which was particularly useful in countering a traffic that relied on sea transport. The conjunction of the latter fact with British control of the sea enabled Britain to force fundamental structural changes in the East African Muslim societies without needing to carry out very much *direct* intervention by Britain in the lives of East Africans. Finally, Britain benefited from the consensus of the European states on human rights issues, which prevented other powers from ever going very far in exploiting local anger against Britain's human rights campaign. Whatever factors were at work, they permitted national interest and idealism to coincide to a surprising degree. Perhaps the most striking fact about this period is that the community most injured by the British campaign against the slave trade, Zanzibar, was also the community most open to British influence.

The Lessons of the British Experience

We have now studied the record of a perservering and successful human rights campaign. At this point we can look at the critique of human rights policy that began this essay in the light of the British experience.

The first striking fact is that, contrary to what we might have expected on the basis of our own brief experience, the British campaign was a definite and obvious success. A traffic that caused immense suffering was ended in the Atlantic and reduced to a furtive trickle in the Indian Ocean and Red Sea. This in turn probably assisted the later abolition of slavery in several countries, by shifting the economic basis of slavery and by establishing a climate of moral condemnation of slavery. This success was not one that affected only externalities. As we have seen, the slave trade was a fundamental part of the social and economic life of societies such as Portuguese Africa, Brazil, and Zanzibar.

This success is, by our expectations, truly remarkable. In several cases it was achieved without the accompanying economic development we often consider necessary for human rights improvement. It is surprising that one great power could develop effective pressure on lesser powers when there were great-power rivalries—to the point of war itself—that could have become involved.

The British campaign against the slave trade was successful in a second sense—that it took place without substantial sacrifice of Britain's national interest. Indeed, the overall relationship may have been in the other direction: Britain's human rights campaign may have increased Britain's international prestige, and its success may have made Britain appear more powerful.

The record of this period seems to contradict the plausible argument that a human rights policy will not work because states will not tolerate interference in their internal affairs. In the climate of the nineteenth century countries such as Portugal, Brazil, and Zanzibar were often irritated by interference in their domestic lives but were unable to protest it effectively; in the end they did not complain very much.

It was an important limitation of the British campaign that it did not attack—until quite late—slavery itself. Aside from this, Britain's human rights policy made few concessions to the diversity of circumstances and traditions in the areas where it attempted to abolish the slave trade. Historically, the movement to abolish the slave trade arose from English and French natural rights thinking of the seventeenth and eighteenth centuries—a way of thinking rather alien to Mediterranean Europe, Latin America, and the Islamic world. In some Muslim countries resistance to this campaign was presented (rather questionably) as a principle of loyalty to Islamic law. Although the British human rights policy failed to make any substantial concessions to this diversity, this does not seem to have interfered greatly with its effectiveness.

There is one clear difference between Britain's human rights campaign and the atmosphere surrounding U.S. human rights policy during the Carter years. The period of greatest activism on human rights was a period of relative U.S. withdrawal from its maximum world role and of self-restraint in the increase of military power. Though a widespread climate of opinion in the 1970s saw both a human rights policy and the limitation of U.S. national power as manifestations of idealism, Britain's experience in the nineteenth century suggests that these two principles are really in contradiction with one another.

The simplest way in which British power supported the British human rights campaign was by coercing human rights violators. In Brazil, in Zanzibar, and in Persia the decisive decisions to abandon the slave trade were directly produced by British use of military force, or the threat of it, which these countries were too weak to resist. British economic power—the dependency of many such nations on British investment and trade—prevented British action from being crippled by fears of retaliation by the nations affected.

But probably more important than these direct effects of British power was the influence of the British example. Of all the major powers in the nineteenth century Britain was the nation that most stood for human rights principles. It is difficult to account for Britain's success in advancing these principles without considering how Britain's success in the world must have been seen by other nations as a result, at least in part, of its principles. No nation's insistence on human rights can have a powerful effect if that nation does not provide an example of the success of those principles. A weak, poor, and despised nation cannot provide an attractive example.

In recent years the United States sometimes seemed to base its human rights policy on the opposite assumption. In his Notre Dame speech defining his new human rights emphasis, President Carter declared that "through *failure*, we have now found our way back to our own principles and values."[62]

British willingness to use power in ways that are now shunned appears to have been a precondition for the success of her human rights policy. When looking back at the nineteenth century, we tend to approve the moral concerns of Britain but to condemn her pugnacity and lack of respect for others' rights. But a close examination of the history suggests that the latter may have been a necessary means for the success of the former. In pursuing her policy against the slave trade Britain was willing to use force and to intervene in other nations in ways that appeared to infringe their sovereignty and equality. Lord Palmerston was able to deal effectively with the Portuguese slave trade from her colonies to the New World only when he secured passage of a bill allowing Britain to seize Portuguese ships without the consent of Portugal and to try them in British courts. Portuguese slave ships were seized in Brazilian harbors, and slave depots on the African coast were destroyed by the Royal navy. When the treaty of 1817 expired, the Aberdeen Act was passed, and Brazil was treated the same way as Portugal had been. The slave trade to Brazil was finally crushed, in 1850–51, only after the British navy began seizing and burning slave ships in Brazilian harbors, with "magical" effect.

Similar measures were most effective in ending the East African slave trade. In 1847 Palmerston forced Iran to ban the slave trade by threatening to seize slave ships without any treaty. Later he did mandate the searching of Persian ships without Persian consent. In Zanzibar, as in Brazil, the end of the traffic finally came when Britain began seizing Zanzibari slave boats passing between various parts of Zanzibar's territory and compelled a treaty by the threat of a total blockade. As the British consul declared, he had come to dictate, not to discuss.

Elements of a Successful Human Rights Policy

There is a further respect in which the British human rights policy differed from recent U.S. policy. The latter has been substantially influenced by the feeling that Third World nations have a right to develop in their own way without strong influence from the West. These principles have a genuine dignity. There was an arrogance in Britain's high-handed proceedings that now seems ugly to us. But this should not prevent us from noticing that a real contradiction exists between an activist human rights policy and the principle that strictly forbids all interference with the internal life of other sovereign states.

It follows from what we have argued, and what can be observed in the history of the British human rights campaign, that there were two forms of high principle that could only act to impede that campaign: pacifism and legalism. Opposition to coercion and respect for law were strongly rooted in Britain. The former only created an opposition to the way the campaign against the slave trade was carried out, but the decrees of judges several times hampered it seriously. Rigid adherence to international law would have ruled out most of the decisive acts against the slave trade because those acts had the character of arbitrarily allowing Britain to judge acts done by citizens of other states.

A further precondition for the success of the campaign against the slave trade was that Britain undertook to do a great deal but not too much. Britain fought the slave trade strongly but not slavery itself. Yet the campaign against the slave trade contributed a great deal to extinguishing slavery at a later time. This suggests two principles for future human rights efforts. First, it suggests that a separation should be made between those abuses that can be remedied with the means available and those that cannot; the former should be attacked with vigor and the latter largely, though not entirely, ignored. Second, an effort should be made to target decisive human rights violations whose elimination will have a catalytic effect on broader abuses.

Two final and very important preconditions are related to less tangible elements of international life. Britain's actions were supported by a consensus among the important powers that the slave trade was an evil. The concrete effect was that other powers generally did not try to exploit the hostility to Britain that the campaign against the slave trade aroused in order to further their own rivalries with Britain. Brazil and Zanzibar appealed to France in vain. At the Congress of Vienna, Prussia, and Russia, the powers most opposed to Britain on political questions, supported Britain on the issue of the slave trade. The result was typified by Brazil, who felt helpless to resist the "torrent" moving against the slave trade.

This kind of international moral consensus exists today in principle; the United Nations is a concrete embodiment of this principle. At first glance we seem to have far more of this kind of consensus than existed in the nineteenth century, when the major powers were open and unabashed rivals and even fought wars against one another without needing excuses such as peace or national liberation. But, strangely enough, the increasing prominence of explicit moral consensus in international life has been accompanied by its real deterioration. The well-known "politicization" of international bodies such as the United Nations Educational, Scientific and Cultural Organization (UNESCO), the International Labour Organisation (ILO), and the World Health Organization (WHO) implies that there is no moral or humanitarian principle that is taken to transcend the advantage of a given side. At present there is virtually no act so revolting that it will not be excused by one state or another.

This lack of consensus today is an obvious limitation on the effectiveness of human rights efforts. Measures that could help recreate an effective international consensus would be an important contribution to international human rights. Any such efforts would have to bear in mind two opposing considerations: A consensus cannot consist, on the one hand, of one nation, but, on the other hand, the attempt to create an absolutely universal consensus is one of the causes of the lack of any effective consensus today.

In the meantime, whatever strengthens the unity of the external environment faced by human rights violators would seem to be useful for human rights. In the nineteenth century an important factor in giving an impression of such unity was the insistence of the major powers that, just as they would not permit slaves to be wronged, they would not be wronged themselves. The nineteenth century was marked by a keener sense of honor than our own. This sense of honor probably contributed to human rights, not only by protecting the rights of some, but by diffusing a general sense of rigid moral standards that could be enforced.

A final precondition of Britain's effective human rights policy itself underlay the consensus of human rights. This was the self-confidence of nineteenth-century Britain discussed earlier. Palmerston could believe that the slave trade, a flourishing economic reality, was "doomed" and that Britain was "the main instrument in the Hands of Providence" in acting against it. This is a very clear difference from recent U.S. policy, which was based to a considerable degree on the sense of American guilt. Ambassador Young said, "I see my country as vulnerable as anybody's else's around the table."[63] Likewise President Carter stated, "We have our own shortcomings and faults. . . . We are determined to deal with our deficiencies quickly and openly . . . *we are ourselves culpable.*"[64] Any measures that assist in the recovery of U.S. and Western self-confidence may lay the foundation for an effective human rights policy.

The situation of Britain in the nineteenth century is so different from our own that we cannot draw simple lessons. We cannot recreate some of the preconditions of British success, and we would not wish to recreate others. Yet we may learn a great deal from the experience of others who carried out a human rights policy with real success.

Notes

1. For a fuller account of the historical evidence, with complete references, see Charles H. Fairbanks, Jr. (with the assistance of Eli Nathans), "The British Campaign Against the Slave Trade as an Example of a Successful Human Rights Policy," in Fred Baumann, ed., *Human Rights and American Foreign Policy* (Gambier, Ohio: Public Affairs Conference Center, 1981). An abridged version of this essay appeared in the Fall 1982 issue of *This World*.

2. Leslie Bethell, *The Abolition of the Brazilian Slave Trade: Britain, Brazil and the Slave Trade Question, 1807–1869* (Cambridge: Cambridge University Press, 1970), p. 16.

3. The main sources used in the following account of the Atlantic slave trade are Bethell, *Brazilian Slave Trade* and Alan Manchester, *British Preeminence in Brazil: Its Rise and Decline* (Chapel Hill, North Carolina: University of North Carolina Press, 1933).

4. Bethell, *Brazilian Slave Trade*, p. 14.

5. Ibid., pp. 4–42.

6. Ibid., p. 8.

7. Harold Temperley, *The Foreign Policy of Canning 1822–1827: England, the Neo-Holy Alliance, and the New World* (London: G. Bell and Sons, 1925), p. 194.

8. Bethell, *Brazilian Slave Trade*, pp. 40, 46.

9. Ibid., p. 39.

10. Ibid., p. 60.

11. Ibid., p. 62.

12. Ibid., p. 78.

13. Ibid., p. 85.

14. Ibid., p. 102.

15. Ibid., p. 105.

16. Ibid., p. 155.

17. Ibid., p. 159.

18. Ibid., p. 180.

19. Ibid., p. 136.

20. Ibid., p. 183.

21. Ibid., p. 153.

22. Ibid., p. 297.

23. Ibid., p. 333.

24. Ibid., p. 338.

25. Ibid., p. 338.

26. Ibid., p. 351.

27. Ibid., p. 363 (emphasis added).

28. Ibid., p. 217.

29. Ibid., p. 362.

30. Christopher Lloyd, *The Navy and the Slave Trade: The Suppression of the African Slave Trade in the Nineteenth Century* (London: Longman, 1949), p. 148.

31. Bethell, *Brazilian Slave Trade*, p. 374 (italics in the original).

32. Ibid., p. 307.

33. Ibid., p. 308.

34. Robert Conrad, *The Destruction of Brazilian Slavery 1850–1858* (Berkeley: University of California Press, 1972), p. 22.

35. Bethell, *Brazilian Slave Trade*, p. 341.

36. Ibid., p. 308.

37. *Country Reports on Human Rights Practices for 1979*, Report Submitted to the Committee on Foreign Affairs, U.S. House of Representatives, and the Committee on Foreign Relations, U.S. Senate, 4 Feb. 1980, pp. 1–2; *Country Reports* [for 1980], 2 Feb. 1981, p. 2; cf. p. 4.

38. Manchester, *British Preeminence in Brazil*, p. 317.

39. Ibid., p. 221.

40. The following discussion of the campaign against the East African slave trade is drawn primarily from the following sources: J. B. Kelly, *Britain and the Persian Gulf, 1795–1880* (Oxford, Clarendon Press, 1968); Reginald Coupland, *The Exploitation of East Africa, 1856–1890: The Slave Trade and the Scramble* (London: Faber and Faber limited, 1939); R. W. Beachey, *The Slave Trade of Eastern Africa* (London: Rex Collings, 1976); Lloyd, *Navy and the Slave Trade*, and Suzanne Miers, *Britain and the Ending of the Slave Trade* (London: Longman, 1975).

41. Kelly, *Britain and the Persian Gulf*, p. 423.

42. Ibid., pp. 426–29.

43. Ibid., p. 443.

44. Ibid., p. 448.

45. Ibid., p. 583–84.

46. Ibid., p. 583.

47. Ibid., p. 602.

48. Ibid., p. 586.

49. Ibid., p. 599.

50. Ibid., p. 608.

51. Ibid., p. 620.

52. Miers, *Ending of the Slave Trade*, p. 89.

53. Coupland, *Exploitation of East Africa*, p. 133.

54. Kelly, *Britain and the Persian Gulf*, p. 630.

55. Coupland, *Exploitation of East Africa*, p. 89.

56. Lloyd, *Navy and the Slave Trade*, p. 265.

57. Coupland, *Exploitation of East Africa*, p. 209.

58. Ibid., p. 230.

59. Ibid., p. 242.

60. Ibid., p. 231.

61. Ibid., p. 266.

62. President Jimmy Carter, Commencement Speech at Notre Dame, 22 May 1977 (emphasis added).

63. Ambassador Andrew Young, Speech to the United Nations, 17 March 1977.

64. President Jimmy Carter, Press Conference, 23 February 1977 (emphasis added).

4

Affirmative Action: Human Rights at Home

Fred Baumann

Among the Carter administration's proudest accomplishments was raising the issue of human rights to the forefront in its foreign policy. Leaving aside the host of questions about the execution of that policy, making human rights an issue seems to me just cause for pride.

Human rights are universal because they claim to apply to all men as men. Moreover, it is a striking fact of contemporary politics that this claim to universality is accepted, at least in the abstract, even by the worst tyrants of the day. Human rights, however, are the particular product of our own tradition; they are part of the inherited custom and natural vocabulary of liberal democracies. To raise the standard of human rights then would be, one would think, to define debate in terms congenial to ourselves and, for once, in a way that meets no direct opposition.

Vigorous efforts are under way in the world, however, to redefine the content of human rights in order to make them more comfortable for the despotisms that pay them lip service. Even Indira Gandhi, who has never yet quite arrived at full-fledged despotism, reportedly once justified in a striking formulation her policy of compulsory sterilization by appealing to the "human right" of the nation to survive. In recent years, Third World nations have been pursuing a policy in UNESCO of establishing support for government control of the press in the name of the right to information. So-called second- and third-generation human rights have been discovered, such as the right to medical care, equality of income, or even peace. This redefinition of the content of human rights has not been the exclusive preoccupation of undemocratic, non-liberal regimes. The American Bar Association (with initial funding from

A somewhat different version of this essay was published in the *St. John's Review* (July 1980).

the Ford Foundation) has established a committee on human rights that sees its purpose as spreading knowledge of and acceptance for the "international" standard of human rights within this country.

The issue of human rights, then, may serve as a means for liberal democracies to hold the conduct of all nations to their own traditional standards. The issue of human rights may also be a vehicle for transforming the principles and self-understanding of liberal democracies themselves. Liberal democracies, by defining themselves in terms of the rights they protect, differ fundamentally from other kinds of regimes, traditional or modern. For the United States, the seminal documents of our polity—the Declaration of Independence and the Bill of Rights to the Constitution—root themselves in concepts of human rights. The famous Declaration of the Rights of Man and Citizen of 1789 is the foundation not only of French but of all continental European liberalism and even social democracy. It is also the titular referent for the Universal Declaration of Human Rights, which is now the text that United Nations debates and resolutions on human rights undertake to gloss. Although human rights claim and are claimed by all, we are their special familiars. If they are changed fundamentally, then so are we.

The redefinition of human rights in the United States to meet the "international" standard is, however, by no means simply an accommodation to the countermeasures of nonliberal nations defending themselves against the painful imposition of liberal standards. In at least one crucial respect—affirmative action—we have, completely on our own initiative, undertaken to redefine the content of human rights in a radical way. (For present purposes, affirmative action simply means preferential treatment in selection for places on the basis of race, religion, ethnic group, or gender. It does not here mean "quotas" or "goals" or "underutilization studies" or "special recruitment efforts," all of which play a role in its ungainly structure.)

This redefinition of human rights did not come about suddenly but in timid, gradual steps that long concealed its fundamental character. Consequently, the whole subject of affirmative action, not least its name, chokes in euphemism, jargon, and exoteric language. Some of this evasive language arose through misunderstanding and careless thought. Some of it, I believe, was purposefully devised to mislead.

To define affirmative action as preferential treatment is unlikely to shock anyone. But it is worth remembering that even eight years ago it would have been highly controversial. Eight years ago still, the supporters of affirmative action (especially public officials) denied that affirmative action involved preference. If they did not get angry at those who said it did involve preference, they would pity their naivete.

The case of Allan Bakke, decided in 1978, marked a turning point in the argument. A white, Bakke sued the University of California Medical School at Davis, claiming racial discrimination. The case involved the clearest sort of preferential treatment, because black applicants were treated separately as a group and judged by lower standards than white applicants. Despite the previous general denial that affirmative action involved preference, most defenders of affirmative action took the line that a decision favorable to Bakke would mean the end of affirmative action, including those forms where preference was not, or was less clearly, involved. As a result of the discussion surrounding the Bakke case, the fiction that affirmative action did not actually involve preference was wholly exposed and consequently, for the most part, quietly dropped.

In the *Bakke* case and the *Weber* case that followed it in the next year, the Supreme Court was faced with a fundamental constitutional question that, given the dependence of the Constitution and the Bill of Rights on assumptions about human rights, was also a fundamental question of human rights: Can preferential treatment by skin color be brought into harmony with the right to equal treatment by the laws? The specific constitutional arguments of due process and equal treatment have been rehearsed in hundreds of amicus briefs and scores of articles. To cast some light on the more general perspective of human rights, let us take the admittedly artificial step of consulting a non-American document, the Declaration of the Rights of Man and Citizen, the grandfather of the present "international" standard of human rights.

Article 1 of the Declaration says that "men are born and remain free and equal in rights." Article 2 holds that "the aim of every political association is the preservation of the natural and imprescriptible rights of man." These rights, it says, are liberty, property, security, and resistance to oppression. Since everyone's rights must be protected, they must be protected to the same degree. Consequently, law, we learn from Article 6, "must be the same for all whether it protects or punishes. All citizens, being equal in its eyes, are equally eligible to all public dignities, places and employments, according to their capacities, and without other distinction than that of their virtues and their talents."[1]

Equal Opportunity vs. Affirmative Action

Equality before the law remains the core of the traditional democratic position on the rights of citizens. It was the fundamental argument of the U.S. civil rights movement from Frederick Douglass to the passage of the Civil Rights Act of 1964 (and in many cases, thereafter as well). The principle of equality before the law not only gave the movement an unshakeable confidence in the justice of its cause but also paralyzed the will and conscience of its opponents, themselves liberal democrats with a "But." Equality before the law seems to rule out all forms of race, sex, ethnic, or religious preference in selection, no matter what the excuse. The principle of equality before the law remains, for principled liberal opponents of affirmative action, an arsenal of telling theoretical and practical arguments. These arguments do not tell because they are self-evidently true. Many nations and teachings would find artificial and even bizarre the intellectual context from which they emerge. These arguments tell because they *appear* self-evidently true, because most of the proponents of preference, themselves liberal democrats with a "But," agree, or think they agree, with them in principle.

Obviously, in relying on theories of natural rights, the Declaration of the Rights of Man, like the Declaration of Independence and the Bill of Rights, depends on assumptions one need not share. Perhaps there are no such things as "natural and imprescriptible rights." Consequently, perhaps civil society has some other character than a mechanism designed by men to assure themselves of the maximum feasible exercise of these natural rights. Perhaps the state is merely the formal expression of the particular phase of the class struggle that has been reached, or perhaps it is the formal expression of a nation's eternal racial character. If it is, then we know that the "bourgeois rights" defined by the two Declarations will find themselves swiftly relativized and superseded by the supreme right of class or race, represented customarily by the even more supreme right of the party leadership. That is, to the extent that these rights continue to be respected, they will be justified as furthering the class struggle or the race's strength, not as expressing those natural and imprescriptible rights of the individual that the regime teaches are a naive and malignant myth. And of course, although these totalitarian alternatives to human rights liberalism have been among the most striking ones in this century, many other nonliberal alternatives are possible as well.

In this country, however, the Civil War may be said to have settled in principle that the words of the Declaration of Independence meant what they said about the created equality of all men. The United States of America was the first nation founded on an abstract principle, though a principle made increasingly less abstract by the United States' very existence, namely that a state is not the political organization of a people but rather an organization that allows individuals to fulfill their natures and, more specifically, to exercise their natural rights of life, liberty, and the pursuit of happiness. It is thus worth recalling that the identity of citizenship and membership in a people was in fact precisely the principle of those who fought against the equality of black and white in the United States. As a group of South Carolina whites protested to Congress in 1868: "The white people of our State will never quietly submit to negro rule. . . . We will keep up this contest until we have regained the heritage of political control handed down to us by honored ancestry." They owe this duty, they say, to their land and their "proud Caucasian race."[2]

If the outcome of the Civil War retrospectively settled the principled issue of the character of the founding, only the Civil Rights Act of 1964 and the Voting Rights Act of 1965 made fulfillment of the principle in practical reality a likelihood. With its passage, the United States became the nation where citizenship transcended nationality most purely. Although ties of family, language, common ancestry, and culture remained strong (though not quite so strong as in, say, Canada, our multinational neighbor), from 1964 on the United States asked everyone to put aside the advantages of group membership and, in the public realm, to take his chances on fair treatment from the great and anonymous society.

Equal opportunity is demanding, involving a great gamble for society because it requires a great gamble from each of its citizens. The demand that people generally live up to their legal and moral responsibilities only becomes feasible if there is strong faith in the reality of equal opportunity. The risks inherent in equal opportunity inspire anxiety precisely about its reality. For along with a powerful interest in equality, there goes at least as powerful an interest to cheat.

Viewed from this perspective, it is hardly paradoxical that in the nineteen years since the passage of the Civil Rights Act there has been a revival, through affirmative action, of group consciousness and group competition. Superficially, it might seem that the American project was simply too ambitious, too frightening, and that affirmative action therefore merely represents a retreat to easier, less just days. The renewed search for legally based group advantage, however, emerged from the thinking of those who imagined themselves most wholly devoted to the principle of equality of opportunity.

In name and purpose, affirmative action was not meant to reaffirm group membership in defiance of the attempt to neutralize it in the public realm. It was understood originally as something vague but extra—a helpful shove to a too-timid liberalism. Lawrence Silberman, one of the chief formulators of early affirmative action policies, when he was employed by the Labor Department in the Nixon administration, described nine years later the anxious desire he had originally shared with his colleagues to find some way to make concrete the abstract equality of opportunity guaranteed by the Civil Rights Act of 1964 and at the same time to avoid the practices of racial preference the Act had rightly prohibited. Silberman and his colleagues had developed "goals" that were meant to be fundamentally different from discriminatory "quotas." These goals, their inventors had asserted, did not legislate preference, but only encouraged attentiveness to the existence of well-qualified minority group members. Nine years later, Silberman concluded that "goals" were indistinguishable from "quotas." He and his colleagues had failed.[3]

Eventually, almost all had to admit that affirmative action, understood as "goals," meant at least some kind of preference, if not exactly "quotas." One could not draw up most favored *ethnoi* lists and urge their selection without making ethnicity a criterion of selection. However genteelly one did it, one lent the authority of the law to discrimination based on ancestry or gender. Interestingly, only a few, like Silberman, drew back in remorse. Most pressed on, seeking to justify preference if it worked in a direction opposite to older forms of preference. Mr. Justice Blackmun, in his dissent in *Bakke*, spoke candidly, if somewhat strangely for a Justice of the Supreme Court:

> I yield to no one in my earnest hope that the time will come when an 'affirmative action' program is unnecessary and is, in truth, only a relic of the past. . . . At some time, however, beyond any period of what some would claim is only transitional inequality, the United States must and will reach a stage of maturity where action along this line is no longer necessary. Then persons will be regarded as persons, and discrimination of the type we address today will be an ugly feature of history that is instructive but that is behind us.[4]

It is not surprising that there was something tentative and uneasy in the formulations of those who came to praise affirmative action as a distasteful but medicinal poison. Not all of Blackmun's utopian posturing and nostalgia for the future could wholly blind him and those who shared his views to the injustice they were doing, according to their own principles, in the present. As a result, the task of justifying affirmative action reached a new stage. The embarrassment of pursuing equal opportunity by discriminatory means suggested the argument that the discriminatory results of these discriminatory means were only apparently discriminatory. Begun without excessive deliberation and meant to be something "extra," affirmative action now began to place a heavy burden on the dialectical skills of its advocates. This was a burden the advocates would in turn pass on to the liberal tradition out of which they came.

The Claims of Utility

The problem was how someone who is *Taking Rights Seriously* (to cite the title of Professor Ronald Dworkin's oft-cited book)[5] could do so and at the same time show that race and sex could legitimately be added to "virtue and talent" as criteria for admission to "public dignities, places, and employments." In response, a number of arguments were adopted that merely begged the question. A typical example was the notion that one could avoid the moral issue arising out of race and gender preference by establishing a minimum for "qualification" so that above that minimum no gradations of merit could apply. Thus, officially, one would not be allowed to know that the better candidate had been denied the position.

A number of other arguments were raised that, however various, in the end all rely on the claim of utility. For instance, it was alleged that the state had a compelling interest in overcoming the de facto separation of the races or the underrepresentation of women; or that minority group members needed role models from their own groups in places of respect and authority; or that there is urgent need for professional services in the inner city that only minority professionals can reasonably be expected to supply. These arguments coexist fairly comfortably with Blackmun's hope for the merely transitory character of affirmative action but rely not just on hope but on the claim of utility.

Arguments based on utility must be addressed at two levels. First, they must be correct on their own terms. Not only must the advocated policy actually produce the intended results, but those results must actually be beneficial, given the general standard of social utility the advocate adopts. Second, every regime, by its fundamental laws and traditions, erects a standard of what is right and seemly. If the means suggested to achieve the social utility the advocate wants violate the standard, then it must be shown that this violation is less important than the good that is being done. This can, of course, be done in two ways: first, by emphasizing the comparative urgency and benefit of the advocated policy; second, by denigrating the worth of the regime's inherent standards of what is right and seemly.

A strong case has been made that the arguments for the utility of affirmative action do not even meet the first set of tests. Some of the most powerful and striking counterarguments have been made by black scholars like Thomas Sowell and Walter Williams. In a paper presented to the United States Civil Rights Commission and later published in a revised form in the *Public Interest*, Professor Sowell demonstrated that in universities—the chief target of affirmative action enforcement in the early 1970s—great advances toward equality, in terms of salary and representation, occurred among faculty between the passage of the Civil Rights Act of 1964 and the advent of affirmative action around 1971, whereupon, for whatever reason, these advances ceased.[6] The evidence of these writers suggests that the factual premise of affirmative action—that equality of representation and living standards could not come about given mere legal equality of opportunity—may not have been correct. Critics (and even advocates) of affirmative action now point out that in many areas the chief beneficiaries of affirmative action have not been members of the group whose plight inspired affirmative action and seemed to justify it—blacks—but women and, in particular, middle-class women. For critics like Professor Sowell, the price in cynicism, revived racial hostility, and apparent confirmation of paternalist racial stereotypes typified by the thought that blacks cannot make it on their own and must be given something is far too much to pay for the few marginal rewards that affirmative action offers its "beneficiaries."

I share the critics' views on this point. Given the fact that affirmative action, by moving beyond the abstract standard of the Fourteenth Amendment and the Civil Rights Act, involves an ever more active governmental intervention in and interpretation of the attainment of concrete equality of opportunity, and given as well the fact that the groups that are to be the beneficiaries of affirmative action are still relatively weak in American politics, one would think that the long- and even middle-term dangers of preference would outweigh its short-term charms to those primarily concerned with the interests of those groups. For what may be given by the strong to the weak as an act of policy may also be taken away. If no generally accepted moral or constitutional principle remains to prevent it, even more than was given may be taken away.

But granting for argument's sake that affirmative action really does aid its intended beneficiaries, does it meet the test of not violating the principles of the American regime? At first sight, it might seem to do so, given the identification of the American regime with the principles of the Declaration of the Rights of Man and Citizen. Article 1 of the Declaration says that "social distinctions can only be based on public utility."[7] The betterment of previously oppressed and victimized groups seems self-evidently to promote public utility in the United States. Therefore, affirmative action would seem not to conflict with our fundamental principles. But although our sense of the self-evident justice and practical benefits of the claimed results of affirmative action clearly betokens affirmative action's origins in a characteristically liberal, characteristically American outlook, it does not settle the question whether the means whereby those results are achieved do not conflict with our most fundamental principles. When the Declaration of Independence speaks of natural and inalienable rights to life, liberty, and the pursuit of happiness, or when Article 2 of the Declaration of the Rights of Man says that the aim of all political associations is to preserve the natural and imprescriptible rights of man, they state those fundamental principles. These are the preservation of rights including, of course, the right of equal treatment by the laws. Unless it can be shown that the race and gender preference involved in affirmative action does not violate these fundamental natural rights, affirmative action conflicts with the most basic principles of the regime, no matter how attractive the benefits of equality and harmony it promises. The claims of utility, understood as material advancement and greater social equality, cannot by themselves carry the day. Their advocates must show either 1) that the necessary means do not, *despite appearances to the contrary*, violate the right to equal treatment by the law; or 2) that the violation is outweighed by the benefits; or 3) that the violation is itself a good thing, or at least a matter of indifference, because the principles are not worth defending.

Utility vs. Fundamental Principles

Let us take the easiest argument, the second in the list, first. If one admits, like Justice Blackmun, both that the natural rights standard is a good and important one and that affirmative action does violate it, how good must affirmative action be to justify the violation? The words "natural and inalienable" and "natural and imprescriptible" of the two declarations suggest the obvious answer: There is no immediate good that justifies the alienation from citizens of inalienable rights. Or, at best, there is only one. If the regime that is the living embodiment of these rights is mortally threatened and can be preserved as the preserver of these rights only by a unique violation of them, then perhaps such a violation would be justified. Lincoln's suspension of *habeas corpus* during the Civil War could perhaps be justified as violating the Constitution in order to save it. Clearly, no such case may be made for racial quotas.

But may it not be the case that rights, though fine and socially useful things, are not really "natural and imprescriptible," and that therefore a much weaker standard of measurement may be adopted for calculating the harm done to the principles of the regime by affirmative action? Here we must recall the theoretical origins of rights. Only then will it become clearer why the right of equality before the law is peculiarly important to liberal regimes and to those who accept their fundamental premises.

Living amid the rich intellectual complexity of traditional societies, where religious, feudal, and national strands of argument and allegiance intermingled, the great theorists of modern natural rights, Hobbes, Locke, and Rousseau, brought a remarkable abstractness of perspective to the subject. They looked beyond the welter of passionate and conflicting allegiances of their times to a natural state where men were and states were not. These apolitical, natural men are dominated by their most fundamental desires. To these desires correspond their natural rights. The right to life is for Hobbes and Locke natural and imprescriptible because, as a rule, the desire to survive is the strongest and most basic desire. But if man wants life, then consequently he must want the means to assure himself of survival. Therefore, liberty, the liberty to assure oneself of the means to live, is also a natural right. But whereas these natural rights are not limited by any government in the state of nature, their actual fulfillment is severely limited by nature itself. These desirous men, therefore, come together to construct civil society as a mechanism that is to assure each of them much of what they want in and by nature. The right to equal treatment and equal opportunity is thus derived from the natural liberty to provide for oneself. It assures men they have not been singled out for special deprivation in exchanging their natural rights for their political equivalents.

If the right to equal treatment, although derivative, is grounded in natural and inalienable rights and is in fact the chief guarantor of the acceptability of a society's founding principles and of its claim to be just, then it is plain that a law that violates equality before the law does enormous damage to that society's legitimacy. If, in contrast, the rights that citizens enjoy do not correspond to natural and inalienable rights that express the most fundamental desires of men as men then civil rights themselves lose their compelling power over us. They either have to be allowed to decay as uprooted or have to be replanted on a new ground that either reinterprets nature or abandons it altogether. If the right to equal treatment under law is not grounded in natural and inalienable rights, the very ends that affirmative action seeks to achieve as a matter of self-evident public utility could and would be called into question. For, as argued above, those ends depend upon a standard for utility that is part and parcel of the natural rights tradition.

At the heart of the claim of simple utility (utility overriding an acknowledged harm to fundamental principle) is a failure to take itself seriously enough. This is evident when affirmative action is defended as an urgently needed corrective for a basically racist society. Those who argue this, and many do, cannot really mean what they say. For in order to mean it, they must actually believe that the consent for equal treatment for minorities like blacks is so solid that not even laws mandating preferential treatment for blacks will imperil it by arousing resentment from the majority whose members are passed over. If the advocates of this view genuinely feared, as I do, that the consent to across-the-board equal treatment (much less affirmative action) is by its very nature fragile, they could hardly be oblivious to the possible consequences of laws that violate equality of opportunity in the name of equality of opportunity (at least to all appearances) and that thus inevitably damage the very name of civil rights and equality of opportunity. The actions of such advocates bespeak a blind confidence in the tractability of the majority before laws that disadvantage them, while their words accuse them of the very opposite, of racism.

The Argument for Compensation

In view of the weakness and self-contradiction of the simple appeal to utility, it is not surprising that the case for affirmative action has had to go beyond Blackmunian admissions of a conflict toward an attempt to demonstrate that the preference involved in affirmative action is actually only apparent—or at least that if real, it can be reconciled with the right to equal treatment by the law. A simple version of the reconciliation begins by noting that the law can be the same for all only metaphorically. An agricultural law affects farmers and nonfarmers differently and affects small farmers differently from large. By analogy, perhaps apparent differences of treatment by race may not violate equality. Might not racial preference be in accord with equality of treatment under law?

There is a vital difference between laws whose results apply differently to farmers and consumers and laws that apply differently to races or genders. Professions and occupations, as the words suggest, are chosen; race and sex are not. When we recall the Declaration's familiar description of liberty as the power to do anything that does not injure others, so that "accordingly the exercise of the natural rights of each man has no limits except those that secure to the other members of society the enjoyment of those same rights,"[8] the difference between the two cases becomes clearer. A law that regulates farmers excludes no one, legally, from birth, from trying to be a farmer. By contrast, a law that regulates selection to schools by race fundamentally limits an individual's opportunities legally and from the outset. It creates places for which it is impossible for some to compete. That is, it violates the natural right to pursue happiness. For the right to pursue must be just that, the right to pursue. It cannot be the right to attain, for the right of one to attain must be the denial to another of the right to pursue. Whereas an agricultural law establishes rules for a competition that the law prevents none from entering, a law entailing racial preferences establishes rules that prevent some from competing and thus from exercising their natural right to pursue, to act.

Consequently, another argument is sometimes advanced that seeks, while staying well within the bounds of traditional liberal assumptions, to demonstrate that the preference inherent in affirmative action is actually in harmony with equal treatment by and before the law as normally understood. This is the argument for compensation. This argument begins with the observation that any definition of equal treatment by the law must include the principle of compensation for suffered injustice. Thus, knowingly to fail to compensate where compensation is possible is to conspire in the perpetuation of unequal treatment. Here it is usually interjected that arguments for compensation are beside the point because it is necessary to know who, specifically, has been injured and how much and by whom before compensation may justly be gauged. In other words, individuals can be compensated for known sufferings, but a group, many of whose members may not have suffered and hence may not deserve compensation, cannot as such be the object of compensation.

The argument for compensation, however, seeks to surmount this obstacle. If we know, as a matter of statistical probability, that most of the members of a definable group suffered a particular injury, then compensation may be in order. Although it is true that the effort to compensate every member of the group will lead to some inequity, because some will have no title to compensation or less title than others, there is still no excuse for failing to make the effort because to do so is to leave known injuries uncompensated.

Getting down to cases, the argument asserts that blacks in the United States have traditionally suffered from violation of their rights and have not enjoyed equal treatment under the law. Perhaps since 1964 blacks may have enjoyed equal legal rights; nonetheless, it is the heritage of the historical deprivation of rights—slavery, peonage, and Jim Crow—that accounts in large part for the overall deprivation of the black population today and that hence makes merely formal equality of opportunity inadequate to create real equality. Consequently, the principle of compensation demands that blacks as a group obtain special advantages and, in particular, preferential treatment. Thus the apparent violation of equal treatment is in fact the fulfillment of equal treatment, and hence no threat is posed to rights of any kind, civil, natural, or human.

At the outset, we may say that this argument carries in its premises some sharply limiting factors. A group, in order to qualify for preferential treatment, must, it seems, have been the object of legal discrimination by the United States. For only if we are guilty as citizens can we be asked to pay compensation as citizens. As individuals whose ancestors may or may not have enjoyed the advantages of discrimination against minorities, we could only be liable for compensation as individuals. In addition, the group to be compensated must also still be suffering the effects of discrimination. Compensation is for *present* (though inherited) harm suffered by contemporary individuals. Hence, current affirmative action programs can hardly be defended in their present form. Today the U.S. government includes in its list for preferential treatment blacks, American Indians, Orientals, Hispanic Americans, and women. Of these groups, only blacks and possibly Indians fulfill the qualifications. Women and Orientals have suffered legal discrimination but do not, as groups, seem to suffer grave socioeconomic disadvantages as a consequence. Mexican-Americans or Puerto Ricans may compose a severely disadvantaged group, but the main causes of this disadvantage do not seem to have been legal discrimination by the United States.

In addition, advocates of group compensation must concede that their program, however just, involves mechanisms that are repulsive to a liberal society. We will still need what we have recently begun to acquire: legal definitions of membership in the black race or in Indian tribes. There will have to be methods of measuring compliance and preventing fraud, whether these involve inquiries into ancestry or the cruder "visual surveys" that we, along with the Republic of South Africa, currently employ.

Furthermore, supporters of this argument assume the burden of showing that preferential treatment, with all its drawbacks, is the most useful form of compensation available. This first requires demonstrating that blacks, for example, are net beneficiaries of preferential treatment. Then it requires a showing that preferential treatment is better for blacks than a cash settlement or any other kind of suggested compensation, such as, for example, government spending on inner-city education or medical and legal services or housing.

The Illogic of Compensation

Finally, inherent in the argument is the admission that the very principle that motivates it and initiates the preferential treatment program must remain unfulfilled and be ultimately violated. The premise of the move to preferential treatment as compensation is that ordinary equal treatment is insufficiently refined. Unsatisfied with the traditional liberal view that looks only to talents and abilities and ignores their provenance, seeing as a fiction the traditional identification of people of all races and backgrounds merely as citizens, the compensation argument demands attention to the actual historical effect of prior deprivation of rights.

The process of refinement of distributive justice involved here has no logical end, however. May all who claim black ancestry under the meaning of the law (whether measured by skin shade or number of black grandparents) receive the same degree of favor? Or should degree of preference coincide with degree of group membership? Since actual deprivation figures in the admission of groups to the list, shall it also figure in awarding compensation to individuals within that group? The logic of historical group compensation leads, as I believe Daniel Boorstin once suggested, to the prospect of assigning to every U.S. citizen at birth an historical-injustice/compensation quotient that would determine the qualitative value of his citizenship. The point of such a reductio ad absurdum is not of course to warn that something similar impends but to note that the principle whose unfulfillment apparently requires preferential treatment in the form of group compensation is in principle unfulfillable. Thus at some point practicality, whose claims had once been denied on grounds of justice, will again have to assert its sovereignty, when preferential treatment has further approximated true distributive justice. The pursuit of perfect justice by means that appear arbitrary and unjust will itself ultimately have to admit that even such means do not attain its end.

The attractiveness of the compensation argument lies in its claim to avoid problems of right altogether. Where the simple utility argument naively admits a conflict between the good of society and some individuals' rights, the compensation argument claims to have found a formula whereby utility may be pursued without endangering the rights of all those who are not given preferential treatment. How is this possible?

It is apparently possible because the compensation argument links, in a double connection, right and interest. It creates no new right to preference. Rather it asserts that where past deprivation of *right* has led to current deprivation of *interest*, or *circumstance*, current preference in *right* is justified if it leads to future improvement in *interest* or *circumstance*. Simply to assert that preference is all right if it benefits the deprived would clearly not advance the argument from the simple utility positions; it would in fact be a retreat. Thus it must be crucial to the compensation argument that it is deprivation of right, not merely material deprivation, that is being compensated. Material deprivation is a necessary condition for obtaining preference, and material improvement is the sought-for end, but it is prior deprivation of right that justifies the apparent (though actually compensatory) deprivation of others' rights now.

Having factored out, as it were, the issue of material deprivation and benefit, it now becomes possible to ask whether there is such a thing as compensation at the level of right. If one has been deprived of goods, they may be returned, perhaps with use penalties added. If one has been deprived of rights, one may be given the fullest possible rights. These rights are limited, as the Declaration of the Rights of Man tells us, by nothing except those limits "that secure to the other members of society the enjoyment of these same rights." What does it mean to be compensated in rights beyond this enjoyment of full civic rights?

Evidently, it would mean to receive the enjoyment, not only of one's own rights, but of the limitation of others' rights. And to that, there can be no right—if only because by enjoying that supposed right, one actually loses one's own. For the intended beneficiary of the limitations of the rights of others endangers his title to his own rights when he endangers the claim of others to theirs. Instead of holding a right to equal treatment that may be claimed before the law and against the state, now both beneficiary and victim of "compensatory" preference owe their legal positions to a political-administrative determination that is perfectly reversible in principle and quite possibly in fact. The security of fundamental rights, a security that is a practical because cultural reality, is lost, and politics becomes a fierce and unlimited struggle of groups for legal recognition and entitlements. Thus the compensation argument turns out to be no improvement on the claim of simple utility, to which it ultimately reduces.

The desire to compensate by manipulation of rights turns out to succeed only at the cost of emptying the notion of rights of its original content. That is, once rights are understood as the expression of the basically active, energetic nature of man, they compel a recognition and an acceptance that makes such interference illicit. Once men are conceived of as fundamentally striving beings who accept the necessary limits of civil society in order to pursue their activities more securely, it becomes very difficult to mount a satisfactory challenge to the use of accomplishments, virtues, and talents as the only legitimate standards for selection. It will appear a fundamental injustice to check some and not others in the pursuit of their activities, unless they are thereby preventing others from acting. (We must keep in mind here that acting means competing for a place, not enjoying it.)

Reinterpreting Natural Rights

Because of the great difficulty of arguing for selection on the basis of race and gender instead of ability and talent within the framework of our inherited thinking about rights, there have recently been attempts to reinterpret natural rights doctrines in a radical fashion to allow the use of racial criteria in selection. Unlike the compensation argument, which tries to show the harmony between preference and traditional notions of right, these arguments turn to those traditional notions and seek to enlarge them to encompass preference.

In *Taking Rights Seriously*, Ronald Dworkin devotes a chapter to the case of Marco DeFunis, the forerunner of *Bakke*. Dworkin desires to refute the traditional liberal position, argued in the *DeFunis* case in the classic brief *amicus curiae* by the late Alexander Bickel of Yale and his University of Chicago colleague, Philip Kurland, on behalf of the Anti-Defamation League of B'nai B'rith.[9] Bickel and Kurland argue that discrimination against a white because he is white is legally indistinguishable from discrimination against a black because he is black.

DeFunis, who was excluded from consideration for a number of admissions places in the University of Washington Law School, was therefore denied equal treatment by the law as much as if a black had been denied consideration because he was black.

In reply, Dworkin separates equality of treatment into two parts: "equal treatment" and "treatment as an equal."[10] Kurland and Bickel think DeFunis deserved equal treatment. Actually, he only deserved treatment as an equal, because treatment as an equal turns out to be our deepest natural right. What then are "equal treatment" and "treatment as an equal?" Their names are similar, but they are sharply opposed in content. Put with excessive crudeness, equal treatment gets you just that, equal treatment, but treatment as an equal plus seventy-five cents now buys you a ride on the crosstown shuttle. Less crudely, "treatment as an equal" means "the right to be treated with the same concern and respect as anyone else," a right that does not, however, extend to immunity from exclusion on grounds of race.

Dworkin's immediate explanation sounds familiar. In an article in the *New York Review of Books*, "Why Bakke Has No Case," he denies that the use of the racial standard is in principle different from use of the standard of intelligence or, in the case of a basketball player, skill.[11] None are chosen qualities and whoever is excluded by the criteria of these qualities may be being excluded not by prejudice "but because of a rational calculation about the socially most beneficial use of limited resources" for medical education.[12] Only if racial classification expresses contempt for the excluded group as a group is it illicit.

Here Professor Dworkin seems merely to suggest another version of the utilitarian argument, already ruled out. We stand once again before the question of the standard of utility. If, on one view of the social good, it is permissible to discriminate in favor of blacks, may not another view of the social good make it possible to discriminate against them? How would one choose between these conflicting views of the social good? Neither would appear to be rooted in the natural and inalienable rights of man.

Aware that utilitarian arguments could be turned against him, Dworkin seeks to ground his view of the innocence of "reverse discrimination" on something stronger than utility (and concedes, by the way, that without this grounding the criterion of contempt also falters). At this point, the right to treatment as an equal, to equal respect and concern, comes into its own. For Dworkin has discerned in John Rawls and adopted from him the "deep theory" that the fundamental natural human right is equality,[13] in the sense of a right to equal "concern and respect in the design and administration of the political institutions that govern" us. For Dworkin, equality is not, as in the Declaration of the Rights of Man, a derivative because postcontractual right, a civic right designed to guarantee the contract and justly to distribute the legal capacity to enjoy individual natural rights. In its new meaning it has become the most fundamental, primary, and natural right of all. Consequently, social policies that bring about greater equality, though they may seem to violate the traditional meaning of equal treatment, in fact exemplify its deeper, its natural, content.[14] "Benign" or "reverse" discrimination, which promotes "treatment as an equal" in its result and exemplifies it in its action, may therefore justify itself in terms of this deeper content. Those who would discriminate against a disadvantaged minority like blacks may well raise utilitarian arguments in favor of their policies. They cannot, however, support them with the ideal argument of furthering equality. Reverse discrimination, in contrast, rests on the firm foundation of egalitarian natural right.

In a review of *Taking Rights Seriously*,[15] Thomas Pangle strikes at the root of Dworkin's project when he notes the absurdity of Dworkin's claim to have discovered "natural" rights "through a reflective process that never steps beyond the conventional horizon of contemporary culture." Pangle is right in questioning what is natural—that is, true to nature—about Dworkin's theory of rights. In Dworkin's own view, "the assumption of natural rights is not a metaphysically ambitious one." It requires no more than the hypothesis that "the best political program, within the sense of that model, is one that takes protection of certain individual choices as fundamental."[16] But to demonstrate why *any* individual choices are fundamental and, beyond that, why *particular* choices should be looked on as fundamental, requires enormous "metaphysical ambition" if it is to end in something more than a scheme of the author's wishes. Moreover, one may wonder about the implications of those wishes, since Pangle also rightly suggests that Dworkin's defense of reverse discrimination could equally be used to justify a compulsory program of leveling eugenics, as both policies would seem to be justified by the deep principle of promoting equality.

Equality of Citizens and Equality of Subjects

It seems to me that, in reinterpreting the natural rights tradition to make the conflict between race preference and natural rights seem to be only seeming, Dworkin has fundamentally departed from that tradition in two ways, regarding both form and content.

The natural rights Hobbes, Locke, and Rousseau talked about had to do with the most fundamental drives of men. Because it was folly to oppose those drives, politics had to accommodate itself to natural rights. Despite all the problems Hobbes faced in dealing with obligation, he still thought that the Leviathan was the best possible political arrangement for passionate, unruly, fearful men who above all desired to stay alive. Locke and Rousseau insisted on the natural right of liberty and its recognition by states: Man cannot possibly consent to slavery because he thereby yields control over his very existence to others. Right or wrong, the natural rights teachings of Hobbes, Locke, and Rousseau have power as an account of the world because they rest on assertions about what men are really like and what they really want.

Does Dworkin mean, therefore, when he speaks of a fundamental natural right to equal respect and concern, that, if there is one thing to know about human beings, if there is one irresistible force that drives them, it is their desire to be treated with the same concern and respect as everyone else? Of course not. Yet what then does he mean by calling the wish to be treated with equal respect and concern a "natural" right?

Dworkin defines a right as an interest that men are entitled to protect if they wish. Rights are "not the product of any legislation, or convention or hypothetical contract,"[17] and their status as "natural" comes from an assumption the philosopher makes in order to unite and explain "our political convictions."[18] It is just "one basic programmatic decision." As far as I can tell, Dworkin thinks that a natural right is an opinion, found on examination to coincide with our other political opinions, that a claim to protect a certain interest is simply valid and may not be relativized. It would seem then that Dworkin happens to entertain the opinion of the unquestionable validity of equality. A political thinker like Carl Schmitt, however, might, with equal attention to his own political convictions, assert as a unifying and explicating assumption the unquestionable validity of inequality. In the guise of natural right, Dworkin has reintroduced the very kind of ungrounded claim, based on political opinion, that natural rights theory had tried in the first place to evict in favor of an account of what men are really like. Thus, Hobbes denounced the schools of ancient Greek philosophy because "the natural philosophy of those schools was rather a dream than science and set forth in senseless and insignificant language. . . . Their moral philosophy is but a description of their own passions." He accuses them of making "the rules of *good* and *bad* by their own *liking* and *disliking*," so that "everyone does, as far as he dares, whatsoever seems good in his own eyes."[19]

There is no teaching of right that does not at least imply an understanding of what men are really like. Let us assume that Dworkin is right in asserting that our most fundamental right is obtaining "equal concern and respect in the design and administration of the political institutions that govern" us. What does the assumption of a right to "equal concern and respect" tell us about ourselves and about the "political convictions" that lead us to make that assumption?

We know something of Hobbes's and Locke's natural men. Struggling in labor or in battle with their surroundings, taught by hard experience to set voluntary limits on their actions and on their capacities to compel others and nature to their individual ends, they come cautiously, mistrustfully, to civil society because the exercise of their faculties is life itself to them. Liberty, as much as is compatible with the preservation of life, is understood as natural, irrepressible, and primary. Equality, in contrast, lives in the service of liberty because equality guarantees that liberty to pursue one's happiness and enjoy one's rights will be preserved. What kind of men reverse the order and place equality before liberty?

In contrast with the rights of Hobbes and Locke, which have to do with what men do or want to do—with living, getting, pursuing—the fundamental right to equality, in Dworkin's formulation, is strikingly passive. In contrast to the state of nature in Hobbes, Locke, and Rousseau, where natural men existed without government, in Dworkin's quasi-state of nature government already exists because there men enjoy respect and consideration from government and its institutions. What this government does, we know: It administers. But what do Dworkin's natural men do? Like their cousins, Rawls's unpersoned wraiths, who can only be trusted to choose for themselves when they do not know who they are, they seem curiously insubstantial. These men do not seem to want to *do* anything in particular, except possibly to make sure their neighbors are getting no more or less consideration than they. Who are these good children, these model citizens?

After the workers' revolt in East Berlin in 1953 had been crushed, pamphlets were distributed telling the workers that, having lost the confidence of the government, they would have to work all the harder. Bertolt Brecht, who had returned there from the capitalist United States where he had spent the war, thereupon composed a famous epigram. As the people had lost the confidence of their government, he wrote, might it not be easier for the government to dissolve the people and elect a new one? Dworkin's men, it seems to me, are just the people that such a government would have elected. They are pure political subjects, asking for no more than to be properly arranged, ordered, and regulated. They are the pipedream of the social engineer and the tyrant's delight—bloodless, identical, undemanding, distinguished only serially, in the most administratively convenient way. Auden's "Epitaph on a Tyrant" begins:

> Perfection, of a kind, was what he was after. And the poetry he invented was easy to understand.[20]

Procrustes was such a tyrant, devoted to the aesthetic ideal of symmetry. Here are the citizens of their dreams.

If I am interpreting Dworkin's implicit anthropology correctly, we have learned something about "our political convictions." Equality of opportunity—Dworkin's "equal treatment" and what the Declaration of the Rights of Man means by the standard of virtues and talents in selection—is the concept of equality from the viewpoint of the citizen, the active, living, individual. Equality of respect and consideration—Dworkin's "treatment as an equal" and what others have called equality of result—is the concept of equality from the viewpoint of the ruler. From the citizen's viewpoint, politics fundamentally means deliberating, persuading, and voting. From the viewpoint of the ruler, which Dworkin shares, politics fundamentally means administering, ordering, and manipulating. From that perspective, mere equality of opportunity is too messy: The chips fall where they may, not where you say. Government is called upon to arrange the chips symmetrically in the most aesthetically pleasing way.

The Paradox of American Liberalism

The attempt to fashion a theoretical defense of affirmative action started with a view of affirmative action as only a minor refinement of traditional human rights liberalism. It proceeded from the refinement of equal opportunity liberalism to its abandonment. It then abandoned the natural rights tradition in all but name. From there it proceeded to abandon first liberty and then even politics itself, replacing them with administration. There is something deeply disturbing in the gradual awakening into self-knowledge and self-confidence of this antipolitical politics.

The rejection of the liberal human rights tradition may seem to be a matter of merely academic interest to those who are not liberals. But liberalism has a special importance for Americans.

I spoke of the peculiar abstractness of Locke and Hobbes as they articulated the state of nature. It is an abstractness that has been criticized since Rousseau. Undoubtedly there is something fictional (more fictional perhaps even than the historical status of the state of nature) about the liberal idea, stated in Hobbes and Locke, of what men are by nature and how they come, without race, culture, or prior history, to create in equal partnership a free civil society. But if it is a fiction, it is one of very special significance to us, for it tells our story and has thus, astonishingly, ceased to be in crucial ways a fiction.

The United States is the liberal state par excellence. Precisely through our historical struggle with the question of race, we came close to vindicating our claim to be a state based on the rights of man as man, and not on the history of a particular people. Of course this does not mean that we do not form a people, but rather that, paradoxically, our peoplehood is grounded on liberal ideals, embodied in the Declaration of Independence, and thus on the denial of the primacy of peoplehood. Our history, as Tocqueville knew before Louis Hartz, is the history of liberalism, and our greatest historical test has been living up to liberalism in the hardest case. Unlike the Declaration of the Rights of Man and Citizen, which in some sense is still a partisan document in France, all Americans can take pride in the Declaration of Independence and the Bill of Rights. Assimilation into the American people is relatively easy, not because there is no such thing as an American people, but because liberalism's willful ignorance of men's origins, their family, nation, and religion has allowed assimilation to mean essentially no more (and no less) than becoming a citizen, one with rights who believes in rights along with the citizen's responsibilities these rights imply. This willful ignorance, which Justice Harlan calls the colorblindness of the Constitution, lies at the heart of America's peoplehood, its nationality.

At one point, in his discussion of reverse discrimination, Dworkin astutely observes that the phrase I just cited—the colorblindness of the Constitution—means "just the opposite of what is says: It means that the Constitution is so sensitive to color that it makes any institutional racial classification invalid as a matter of law."[21] Here Professor Dworkin is perfectly right, and he thereby draws attention to the extraordinary daring involved in trying to create and preserve a country where one is limited only by one's capacities in what one attains and not by accidents of birth. His remark also illuminates the necessity of the severity of those restrictions, especially equality before the law, that alone can make such a rash undertaking feasible. A nation of liberal people, based on the principles of the rights of man as man, is a paradox because it makes particularity out of universality (not, as with countless historical peoples, universality out of particularity). That our nation is a paradox of two centuries more or less successful duration makes it only the more, not the less, astonishing. For it is ultimately only by recognizing the fundamental precariousness of our situation, by recognizing how fragile must be the consent to transcend family, race, and heritage, that that precariousness can be prevented from forcing itself on our attention by the breakdown of that consent.

Affirmative action sprang from a contemporary liberalism confident enough of its foundations to forget them and even radically to undermine them for the sake of a temporary and minor structural improvement. By now affirmative action has revealed itself as a straightforward threat to the liberal principles of the rights of man as man. Paradoxically, it is because our paradox, our enduring paradox, no longer seems a paradox, because the transformation of the liberal idea into a liberal people, a liberal nation, has been so successful that that transformation now threatens to be undone. We fall apart into the ancient, pre-American and premodern quarrels of race and sect for the sake of political dominance and possession of the power to promote our own and harm others.

A Failure of Recognition

It would be a mistake to think that the exercises of theorists like Dworkin or Rawls have no correspondence to developments in the political world. The gulf between ruler and ruled, governor and citizen, has become wider on this issue, precisely along Dworkinian lines. Preferential treatment is a deeply unpopular policy, at least according to public opinion polls. According to one Gallup poll, 83 percent of all Americans object to preferential treatment. Strikingly, a majority of the very groups that are the supposed beneficiaries of affirmative action agree with their fellow citizens.[22] But the officials whose job it is to promote and develop affirmative action have not been deflected by this. Consider, for example, a speech given by Dr. Mary Berry, undersecretary for education of what was then the Department of Health, Education, and Welfare, upon her return from a trip to the People's Republic of China in 1977. In that speech she expressed enthusiasm for almost every aspect of Chinese education, including the practice of employing grade-school children at productive manufacturing. She also praised the regime's frank and rational administration of its system of ideological and class discrimination in education, which excludes the children of former "bourgeois" in favor of the children of "untainted" class elements. "In this last respect," she said, "the Chinese are moving rationally and realistically in a field that has led to confusion and near-hysteria here."[23] Her enthusiasm for the discriminatory practices of a totalitarian regime may most charitably, and probably correctly, be interpreted as the frustrated social engineer's envy of her counterpart's freedom to get on with the work, unhampered by the "confusion and near-hysteria" of public opinion. It is as though such officials are coming to the final alternative sketched above: If the violation of natural rights principles cannot successfully be justified by the benefits that it brings, and if the attempt to explain away the conflict also fails, then only the third alternative remains, which is to denigrate or dismiss the tradition altogether. As we see here, in the case of the American political tradition this means denigrating and dismissing not just a particular understanding of rights but political democracy as well.

As Dr. Berry's remarks indicate, there is an intimate connection between our view of ourselves and our view of the world. In the world of the "result-oriented" (to take a term of art from the lexicon of affirmative action regulators), the differences between liberal and totalitarian regimes, although they may not altogether disappear, at least no longer seem fundamental. Consequently, when nonliberal regimes in the forum of the United Nations mount a critique of the inadequacy of the liberal tradition of rights, when new "rights" are discovered and championed, when old rights, such as freedom of the press, receive new meanings diametrically opposed to the old meanings, it appears to be no longer possible to raise questions of principle about the status of these new rights. In fact, such rights as the right to jobs, medical care, and even peace, and the interpretation of the right to a free press as the right of the government to assure itself of favorable press coverage, are not rights at all in the older understanding but rather are entitlements with a double character. At one level they are entitlements of citizens to particular goods; at another they are entitlements of government to assume and exert the power necessary to deliver those goods. The rights of men, when extended sufficiently, thus magically become the rights of governments. The rights of men, established originally as a barrier against absolute rule, become the ideological justification and buttress of absolute rule.

I do not of course contend that affirmative action implies or is leading to absolutism in the United States. I do contend that the argument over affirmative action has made it much easier for us to lose sight of who we are and what those around us are like. A political philosopher of the twentieth century, referring to the great totalitarianisms of the 1930s, observed that "when we were brought face to face with tyranny—with a kind of tyranny that surpassed the boldest imagination of the most powerful thinkers of the past—our political science failed to recognize it."[24] This failure of recognition remains a danger today. It is only increased by self-mystification.

Notes

1. Frank M. Anderson, ed., *Constitutions and Documents Illustrative of the History of France: 1789–1907* (Minneapolis: H.W. Wilson Co., 1908), pp. 59–61.

2. David Herbert Donald, *Liberty and Union* (Lexington, Mass.: D.C. Heath and Company, 1978), pp. 210–11.

3. Lawrence Silberman, "The Road to Racial Quotas," *The Wall Street Journal,* 11 August 1977, p. 14. "I now realize that the distinction between goals and timetables on the one hand and the unconstitutional quotas on the other, was not valid. Our use of numerical standards in pursuit of equal opportunity has led ineluctably to the very quotas, guaranteeing equal results, that we initially wished to avoid."

4. *Regents of the University of California, Petitioner* v. *Allan Bakke,* Opinion of Justice Blackmun, 28 June 1978, pp. 1–2.

5. Ronald Dworkin, *Taking Rights Seriously* (Cambridge, Mass.: Harvard University Press, 1977).

6. Thomas Sowell, "'Affirmative Action' Reconsidered," *The Public Interest,* Winter 1976, pp. 47–65. See especially pp. 54, 57, and 63–64.

7. Anderson, *Constitutions,* p. 59.

8. Ibid.

9. Alexander M. Bickel and Philip B. Kurland, *Brief of the Anti-Defamation League of B'nai B'rith Amicus Curiae,* in the Supreme Court of the United States, October Term 1973, no. 73–235, p. 19. "The Court is, nevertheless, asked here to hold that the exclusion of a non-black applicant from the law school of the State of Washington, solely because of his race, is a valid racial classification. We respectfully submit, that the rule of equality mandated by this Court in *Sweatt* v. *Painter* compels the reversal of the judgment of the Supreme Court of Washington in this case."

10. Dworkin, *Taking Rights Seriously,* p. 227.

11. Ronald Dworkin, "Why Bakke Has No Case," *New York Review of Books,* 10 November 1977, pp. 13–14.

12. Ibid., p. 15.

13. Dworkin, *Taking Rights Seriously,* pp. 180–81.

14. Ibid., pp. 231–39, especially see p. 239.

15. Thomas Pangle, "Rediscovering Rights," *The Public Interest,* Winter 1978, pp. 157–60.

16. Dworkin, *Taking Rights Seriously,* pp. 176–77.

17. Ibid., p. 176.

18. Ibid., p. 177.

19. Thomas Hobbes, *The Leviathan,* Parts I and II (Indianapolis: Bobbs-Merrill, 1958), pp. 6–7.

20. W. H. Auden, *Collected Poems*, ed. Edward Mendelsohn (New York: Random House, 1976), p. 149.

21. Dworkin, *Taking Rights Seriously*, p. 229.

22. "Preference Or Merit," *Measure* (Bulletin of University Centers for Rational Alternatives), no. 42 (April 1977), p. 1. The reference there is to the *New York Times*, 1 May 1977. Sixty-four percent of nonwhites objected to preferential treatment in the poll.

23. Fred Baumann, "Hands Across the Water: Détente at H.E.W.," *Measure*, no. 46 (April–May 1978), pp. 4–5. On 17 November 1977, Dr. Mary Berry gave a lecture in Chicago called "The Chinese Experience in Education: What America Stands to Learn."

24. Lee Strauss, *On Tyranny*, revised and enlarged edition (Ithaca, N.Y.: Cornell University Press, 1968), p. 21.

5

Human Rights in U.S. Policy Toward the Soviet Union

Myron Rush

Those who want to raise the importance of human rights in foreign policy reveal themselves on examination to be relativists, not absolutists. They do not want human rights to be the concern of U.S. policy everywhere. They do not even want U.S. concern to vary according to the gravity or extent of human rights violations. Instead, they want the United States to defend human rights or stand aside according to the effect this will have on their own primary policy concerns.

Thus, some are indifferent to Soviet violations of human rights, while others go even beyond indifference; perceiving the USSR principally as a partner of the United States in the arms control process and in preventing nuclear war, they insist that Soviet violations of the human rights of its citizens, even if widespread or flagrant, ought not to influence U.S. policy or actions toward the USSR.[1] On the other hand, some advocates of containment of the USSR, although they were indignant when President Ford did not receive the most famous victim of Soviet oppression, Aleksandr Solzhenitsyn, vigorously oppose U.S. condemnation of the repressive policies of rightist governments, fearing that this might weaken them and make them vulnerable to Communist-led revolutions.

The original campaign to elevate human rights in U.S. foreign policy did not aim to make them central but developed instead as a kind of sideshow. The human rights campaign of the mid 1970s (particularly from 1973 to 1976) was not directed at the USSR, the chief object of U.S. foreign policy for almost a quarter century, but at recipients of U.S. economic (and military) assistance. The campaign originated not in the executive branch, which has primary responsibility for foreign policy, but in Congress. It culminated in extensive human rights legislation that critically shaped the conduct of foreign policy but made no direct reference to human rights in the Soviet Union because its authors had no real concern about Soviet violations of human rights.[2] This subordination of human rights policy to other policy concerns is generally acknowledged, although not prominently, by those who advocate upgrading human rights in U.S. foreign policy.[3]

There has been a striking exception to those who recognize that the defense of human rights must be subordinate to the more general objectives of foreign policy. The exception, remarkably, was not some zealous private citizen unburdened by official responsibilities, but a president of the United States. President Carter made human rights central in U.S. foreign policy, seemingly with scarce regard for its effect on security and on the other goals of foreign policy. His early pronouncements as president, especially, manifested a universalism, a kind of impartiality in judging human rights violations that was almost superhuman. In his inaugural address, he proclaimed that "human rights must be absolute."[4] Subsequently, in concluding a major foreign policy speech, he announced: "Our policy is designed to serve mankind."[5] He repeatedly insisted that his campaign for human rights was not aimed at the Soviet Union but was directed against human rights violations everywhere.[6] We are trying through various means, he said, "to implement a renewed awareness of the need for human rights in our dealing with all countries."[7] He wanted the United States "to be the focal point for deep concern about human beings all over the world."[8]

Was the human rights campaign more than an expression of the United States of America's fundamental beliefs—would it affect our relations with other nations? There was a new awareness in many countries "of the importance of human rights, at least in dealing with our own country," inasmuch as human rights had been made a fundamental tenet of U.S. foreign policy.[9] President Carter was concerned that he not speak "with a hollow voice, but that the rest of the world" should know that he was strongly supported by the Congress and the people of the United States.[10] What was to be achieved by this preoccupation of U.S. foreign policy with human rights? The president affirmed his strong belief in the power of words.[11] He early expressed confidence that there was "hardly a government in the world right now that's not trying to do a better job on human rights, partially because we have made such an issue of it."[12]

"Almost the entire world leadership is now preoccupied with the question of human rights. . . . [Twenty-five to thirty nations] have made very substantial moves toward enhancing the quality of human rights in their nations."[13] After four months in office, the president could "already see dramatic, worldwide advances in the protection of the individual from the arbitrary power of the state. . . . "[14] "I don't believe that there is a single leader of a nation on Earth today who doesn't have within his or her consciousness a concern about human rights—how do we appear to our own people, how do we appear to observers from other nations?"[15]

Would the president consider drawing back from his human rights campaign in view of the attacks it had brought on him from the Soviet press and even from Leonid Brezhnev personally? No, these attacks were misdirected.[16] Even if the campaign affected the prospects for SALT, he would not desist, because there was no reason for the two questions to become linked. Nothing could shake his determination to persist in his human rights policy with respect to all countries of the world.[17]

A Substitute for Anticommunism

Although the president's more extreme statements about the universalism and potency of his human rights policy often were made at press conferences, his deep commitment to the human rights campaign was also evident in major prepared speeches. One source of this commitment, no doubt, was Jimmy Carter's moralism, his personal commitment to doing the right thing because it was right, not necessarily because it produced the particular ends desired. But although moralism came easily to Jimmy Carter, the will to make human rights central in U.S. foreign policy did not manifest itself until relatively late in his campaign for the presidency, and its initial motivation was at least partly *strategic*. Originally, however, the strategy was directed principally at winning the presidential election and restoring a domestic consensus for U.S. foreign policy rather than at achieving U.S. objectives in international affairs.[18]

Carter's advocacy of human rights satisfied a felt need to find a substitute for the ideology of anticommunism, which had suffered discredit from the outcome of U.S. involvement in Vietnam. This was strongly implied by the president himself in his major foreign policy address at Notre Dame.

> For many years, we've been willing to adopt the flawed and erroneous principles and tactics of our adversaries, sometimes abandoning our own values for theirs. . . . This approach failed, with Vietnam the best example of its intellectual and moral poverty. But through failure we have now found our way back to our own principles and values, and we have regained our lost confidence. . . . We can no longer separate the traditional issues of war and peace from the new global questions of justice, equity, and human rights.[19]

Even apart from Vietnam, anticommunism in U.S. foreign policy had been attenuated by the 1972 policy of détente, particularly as détente was interpreted by President Richard Nixon and Secretary of State Henry Kissinger, who emphasized that the United States sought cooperation with the Soviet Union, not confrontation or conflict. As the suitability of anticommunism as a foundation of U.S. foreign policy came into question, the commitment to defense of human rights promised to provide a needed substitute. It was not reflected on or thought through before winning Carter's public advocacy but was born of a sudden passion, the illegitimate offspring of a practicing politician's expediency and a reborn Christian's moralism.

Because President Carter embarked on his human rights campaign largely for personal and domestic reasons, its adoption was not attended by close examination of how international factors interact with internal ones to influence Soviet conduct on human rights. Soviet responsiveness to Western pressure to permit Jewish emigration in the late 1960s had been greater than anticipated, and this may have led in turn to exaggerated expectations of what Western pressure could accomplish in more sensitive areas of policy. Dissident groups, to the disappointment of many, actually were subjected to *increased* repression by the Soviet government after the 1972 summit in Moscow. This was partly for prophylactic reasons, to limit the damage done by increased contacts with the West, but it was also in response to the stepped-up activity of the dissidents themselves, who hoped détente would shield them from state repression.

Subsequently, the progress of détente did lead to some loosening of control over dissident groups. The Soviet government's incentives for limiting abuse of dissident groups declined, however, as the promise of economic benefits faded and Soviet political offensives in the Third World led to a worsening of relations with the United States. Moreover, the 1975 Helsinki Agreement committing signatories to the observance of specified human rights gave new impetus to the dissident movement by providing an umbrella under which diverse political currents began to come together, thereby raising Moscow's perception of the dangers posed by the movement. Consequently, the very successes of the dissident movement, though they remained limited and were made possible in part by international considerations, led to increased state repression. Soviet policy on Jewish and German emigration, on the other hand, was not so dependent on internal developments and could more readily be adapted to Soviet efforts to influence the policies of Western governments, especially those of the United States and West Germany.

By the last months of 1976, Moscow found it expedient to launch a strong campaign against the dissidents that continued into the early months of the Carter administration. It is evident that President Carter launched his human rights campaign at a particularly inauspicious moment, when Moscow had determined to take strong measures to destroy the dissident movement's potential for growth. If Carter's aim was to move the USSR toward improved observance of human rights, the prospects were indeed dim. But was this Carter's aim?

President Carter did not think through systematically the place of human rights in global U.S. policy or even in U.S. policy toward the USSR. This failure is understandable in view of the complexity of the problem and the intellectual and practical difficulties in contriving a rational policy and implementing it. This is a subject we shall later examine at some length. Here it suffices to observe that the extreme difficulty of the problem encouraged recourse to a simplistic approach and that Carter's human rights policy was grievously handicapped from the beginning by the weakness of its intellectual underpinnings.

The Soviet Response

That the Carter administration would emphasize human rights in U.S. foreign policy toward the USSR, that it would focus on the dissident movement, and that the president would be its chief advocate, was strikingly apparent almost from the beginning. Within a month of his inauguration, Carter had already made public his reply to the letter Andrei Sakharov addressed to him. In the weeks following he received the exiled dissident leader Vladimir Bukovsky in the White House and reaffirmed on several occasions his intention to concern himself with human rights in the USSR and elsewhere in the world. That the Soviet leaders would give way before the president's public campaign on behalf of Soviet dissidents was hardly to be expected.

In the previous year (1976) Moscow, when attacked for violations of human rights by the Western media and by nongovernmental organizations including Communist parties in Western Europe, was inclined to defend its record and, even while engaging in cruel repressive actions, made some unprecedented concessions such as the exchange of Vladimir Bukovsky for the head of the Chilean Communist party, Luis Corvalan. Now, however, Moscow strongly counterattacked. Leonid Brezhnev personally responded to the president's human rights campaign, publicly accusing the United States of interference in Soviet internal affairs. *Pravda* (13 March 1977) warned that the campaign might adversely affect the prospects for the impending SALT negotiations in Moscow. Following the collapse of these negotiations, the USSR encouraged the notion that the U.S. human rights campaign had contributed to the bad outcome. Subsequent Soviet repressive actions manifested a pronounced anti-American twist. Anatoli Shcharansky was accused of committing espionage on behalf of the United States and was linked to a U.S. correspondent, Robert Toth, who was subjected to prolonged interrogation by the KGB. The Soviet aim, in good measure accomplished, was to weaken the communication links between dissidents and Western journalists. Brezhnev himself pursued his confrontation with President Carter on the question of human rights in the USSR, calling in U.S. Ambassador Malcolm Toon to complain that it threatened to impair relations between the two countries.

The tough Soviet stance toward President Carter's human rights campaign apparently led to a weakening of U.S. resolve to persist in it. By October 1977, when the Belgrade Conference to review performance on the Helsinki accords convened, an increase in repressive actions had seriously weakened the Soviet dissident movement. (While the conference was in session, however, the Soviet government was on its good behavior.) Although the United States launched some rhetorical attacks on Soviet human rights abuses at Belgrade, it did not seek to make the Soviets pay a price for these violations in terms of the economic and scientific cooperation called for by other parts of the Helsinki accords. The Soviet leaders had shown that although Carter's human rights campaign could damage the regime's reputation world-wide, it could neither induce nor compel the Soviet leaders to moderate their rule. Moreover, although international publicity previously had helped to protect dissidents who were still at liberty (or, more correctly, had not been incarcerated), this was less true after Carter initiated his human rights campaign. The Soviet government had no difficulty in demonstrating that the U.S. president could not protect the objects of his solicitude.

Earlier, in the spring of 1977, hardline U.S. SALT proposals in negotiations at Moscow had been sharply rejected by the USSR, leading the United States subsequently to soften its position. Similarly, on the question of human rights in the USSR, Soviet counterpressure in the summer of 1977 induced the United States to modify its position. Moreover, U.S. moderation at the Belgrade Conference was not recip-rocated; if anything, the USSR responded by counterattacking more forcefully. Whether or not Carter's initial campaign to defend human rights in the Soviet Union was wise, his failure to persist in it had unfortunate consequences. It appeared to reinforce the Soviet belief that the appropriate response to pressure from Carter, on questions of human rights, SALT, or whatever, was to take an unyielding stance and apply sharp counterpressure. It was a lesson they learned well. Although President Carter sporadically resumed his criticism of the Soviet record on human rights, his forays appeared to have little positive effect on Soviet performance.

An Incoherent Policy

The weak intellectual underpinnings of the Carter human rights campaign were noted previously. A rationally grounded campaign would have required practical deliberations on a series of questions. Assuming that the campaign was not to be pursued universally and uniformly but was to be subordinated to U.S. security interests, what *objectives*, particularly as regards the USSR, was the campaign meant to achieve? What *means* were appropriate to the pursuit of those objectives? In fitting means to ends, what *assumptions* had to be made about Soviet reality? And what *costs* had to be anticipated, in resources and in alternative ends foregone? The answers to these questions did not have to be precise or intellectually elegant; they required only sufficient definition to provide rough guides to action. Yet it does not appear that these questions were seriously asked or given even the imprecise answers that a coherent human rights policy required. According to a Carter adviser, there had been "no specific planning for a particular human rights campaign or program. . . . [Chance things] blew the issue up unexpectedly."[20]

How was U.S. policy toward the USSR to be served by the campaign? In pressing the USSR to observe the human rights of its citizens, was our aim simply to further human rights in the USSR—that is, to *moderate* the Soviet government's policy toward its own people, especially the dissidents? Or was our aim to *weaken* the regime by compelling it to face a dilemma: either to reduce substantially employment of its powerful and effective repressive machinery, thus opening the way for forces that might undermine political stability, or to refuse to do so, thus causing damage to the Soviet reputation in the world? Or finally, was our aim to *transform* the Soviet regime, to make it more democratic (or more in accord with *Russian* traditions) as many of the dissidents hoped to do?

Failure to distinguish among these objectives and to choose among them would make it difficult to find the appropriate means to employ or to integrate the campaign for human rights into overall U.S. foreign policy toward the USSR and in the world at large. The different aims could be reconciled with each other only to a limited degree. If the United States succeeded in weakening the regime this might facilitate its transformation; but if weakness appeared, no doubt the Soviet leaders would move rapidly to overcome it. Similarly, if the United States succeeded in moderating the Soviet government's policy toward the dissidents, this might lead to a weakening of the regime: But if such a weakening threatened, the Soviet leaders assuredly would be quick to respond with renewed repression of the dissidents. Even if the U.S. government could avoid making clear-cut choices about possible objectives, clarity would still be needed as to the order of priorities among them.

The appropriate means to be employed in a U.S. campaign for human rights in the USSR naturally depend on the objective sought. If the chief U.S. aim were to moderate Soviet repressive policies, there would be a need for quiet diplomacy that offered benefits if the USSR reduced the use of repressive means and threatened to impose penalties if it did not. Even so, the Soviet leaders would not relax their pressure on dissident elements sufficiently to satisfy the United States unless they believed this could be done without endangering political stability. Thus, a necessary premise of a human rights policy aimed at moderating Soviet rule is that the USSR has been using excessive means of repression—that it could ease repression safely and might be induced to do so by a utilitarian calculation of U.S.-imposed costs and benefits.[21]

How realistic is such as assumption? In the years following Stalin's death, the Soviet leaders succeeded in greatly reducing their reliance on his terrible repressive machinery without giving rise to lasting political instability, but it is questionable that a substantial further reduction in the use of repression could be undertaken safely. Although the Soviet leaders may exaggerate their need for repression, they have good grounds for pessimism. The easing of repression in the countries of Eastern Europe has often been followed by social disorder and instability.

Moreover, as the growth of the Soviet economy slowed during the past decade, improvements in living standards became less perceptible, and by the mid and late 1970s ordinary Soviet citizens harbored the view (presumably it is objectively inaccurate) that living standards had worsened. Easing repression at a time of growing material dissatisfaction might be politically unwise; in any case, it was not likely to recommend itself to leaders trained in the Stalin school of governance.

Incidentally, if our primary aim had been to foster the observance of human rights in the USSR—as we claimed—it would have been appropriate to commend the USSR for its improved performance (especially during the Nixon and Ford administrations) in observing the human rights of its citizens: in expelling dissidents instead of imprisoning them, in uniting families, and in permitting generally higher levels of emigration. But such commendation would have helped to improve the Soviet reputation in the world. In practice, the United States gave the USSR little credit for easing repression, and when it did so the Soviet Union probably gained little in world opinion. Shortly after his inauguration, President Carter, citing a rise in Jewish emigration in recent months, did credit the USSR with making progress in human rights.[22] Ironically, this was at a time of sharply intensified Soviet repression of the dissident movement. Such commendations of Soviet progress in observing human rights were infrequently earned and rarely conferred.

Attempting to Weaken or Transform the USSR

If the aim of U.S. policy on human rights were to weaken the USSR in world opinion, this might be furthered by exposing Soviet human rights practices to the world; in that case the appropriate means would be loud and stepped-up propaganda rather than quiet diplomacy. Carter's human rights campaign was in fact most effective in focusing world attention on evil Soviet domestic practices, especially the practices of repressing prominent dissidents, restricting emigration, and using psychiatric institutions to silence and punish dissidents. This damaged the Soviet reputation in countries where these practices are abhorred, and it embarrassed partisans of the USSR, including major Communist parties in Western Europe whose need to compete for public support at home required them to condemn these practices. The resulting gains for the United States in the contest for world opinion were not insubstantial, yet they were necessarily limited. Most governments in the world, while they subscribe to human rights in the abstract, employ similar if less effective means in suppressing domestic dissent. Although their people might be favorably impressed by U.S. efforts on behalf of human rights in the USSR, this probably would be conditional on U.S. espousal of human rights in their own countries—a policy that could have (and not infrequently has had) the effect of antagonizing the governments involved. In countries that do not suffer from political oppression, chiefly member states of NATO, public opinion is no longer as ignorant as it once was about the nature of the Soviet regime. On the crucial questions for them—how active a threat to their own security is the USSR and what sacrifices are required to deal with this threat?—focusing attention on the Soviet government's persecution of its own people is unlikely to have great effect.

If the U.S. objective were not to denigrate the USSR in world opinion but to induce improved Soviet observance of the human rights of its citizens in order to weaken it internally, the prospects of success would be exceedingly poor. Any sign of internal weakness stemming from a more liberal policy toward the dissidents would lead to the quick abandonment of such "rotten" liberalism. If the United States were serious about using the human rights issue to weaken the USSR internally, the appropriate means would not be inducements to the Soviet government to liberalize its policies toward the dissidents but instead direct assistance to those whose human rights are violated, especially among the minority nationalities. This is where the USSR is most vulnerable, and a policy of stirring up nationalist animosities directed against the Soviet state would probably have the best prospects of weakening the Soviet regime. In time, such a policy might weaken the USSR, but the costs involved would be heavy, including a serious worsening of U.S. relations with the USSR and sharp repression of the minorities involved. This is not a policy that the U.S. government could undertake lightly, and it is dubious that it could win consensual support from the American people.

What of the third kind of human rights policy, aimed not at weakening the Soviet regime or ameliorating its repressive character but at transforming it? This is what most of the dissidents aim at. They are courageous, self-sacrificing men and women, many of whom have suffered grievously for their convictions and for the ambitions they harbor for their country. Moreover, even in standing up to a Leviathan far more powerful than the one Hobbes described, they have abjured the use of violence or terror.[23] Nevertheless, the fact that they have had to look to the United States for support testifies to their relative weakness and to their isolation in Soviet society. This isolation became increasingly confining as the Soviet government stigmatized the dissidents as disloyal because of the support they received from the Carter government. With the passage of time, the high hopes of diverse dissident groups that the various ideas they propagate would find a resonance among Soviet intellectual groups, especially in the scientific community, have been disappointed. This may not signify that intellectuals are not attracted to these ideas. The Soviet leaders' response to the emergent dissident movement in the late 1960s, however, was to tighten the party's control over scientific and academic institutions, and these measures, backed by the regime's repressive machinery and command of the country's resources, have met with substantial success.

In time, the diverse dissident groups may be able to act as a catalyst for change because the regime faces unsettling political developments in the decade ahead stemming from the slowed growth of the Soviet economy. It is questionable, however, whether the dissidents' capacity to play such a role would be enhanced by support received from a U.S. human rights campaign, which in fact might tend to discredit them. Probably the United States can best encourage progressive developments in the USSR by cultivating its own inner strengths and by resisting Soviet expansionism.

The Problems Facing U.S. Policymakers

Any serious effort to inquire about the proper place that concern for human rights should have in U.S. policy toward the USSR necessarily points up the severe difficulties encountered in trying to make a human rights policy serve U.S. interests. First, there are deep uncertainties involved in dealing with a complex and inadequately understood Soviet reality, especially when attempting to modify it in particular ways with the narrowly limited means available to the United States for effecting its will. But even assuming that we can act on Soviet reality to achieve our ends, can we agree on what the chief end of a human rights campaign should be—whether to *weaken* the USSR, or to *transform* it, or simply to *further the observance of human rights* in the USSR? Can we be confident that the objective we choose, if achieved, would really advance U.S. interests? Assuredly, no government should ask the quarter billion people of the United States to assume the large costs of a global human rights campaign if a serious case cannot be made that it will increase U.S. security in a dangerous world.

Equally serious problems arise in fashioning a human rights policy toward the Soviet-sponsored regimes of Eastern Europe. It is necessary once more to ask: Is our object to weaken, to moderate, or to transform these regimes? If our object is to *weaken* them, the most potent weapon is nationalism, which in Eastern Europe is largely directed against the USSR. Such nationalism is an explosive force, however, one that should not be tampered with lightly. Moreover, if our object is to weaken these regimes, we should recognize that their rulers depend, in the last analysis, on the Soviet Union; when they become more fearful of their own people their dependence on Moscow is increased. Or is our aim to *moderate* these regimes, to encourage their observance of human rights? The leaderships in some of them, as in Poland and Czechoslovakia and perhaps East Germany, might be forced from power were they substantially to moderate their repressive policies, and this is an outcome they would not willingly accept. Other leaderships, as in Hungary, are perhaps as moderate as they dare to be. In either case, a human rights campaign directed at correcting human rights violations in these countries would probably serve little useful purpose.

Is our aim to *transform* these Soviet-sponsored regimes? This they are more likely to achieve, if at all, on their own. Direct efforts to support the forces seeking to transform the East European regimes, although not likely to discredit these groups as such support would in the USSR, would tend to exacerbate repressive action on the part of leaders who generally are predisposed to defend their power at the slightest threat. Moreover, were they reluctant to take repressive action, their patrons in Moscow would surely press them to do so, especially if the United States were actively campaigning for the human rights of advocates of transformation. Soviet forebearance when such transformation is in prospect is in any case unlikely (as Soviet conduct in Hungary in 1956, Czechoslovakia in 1968, and Poland in 1981 made clear), and a U.S. human rights campaign would only worsen the chances. Transformation may yet prove to be a live option for East Europeans willing to take risks to bring it about, but its advocates would receive dubious benefits from a U.S. human rights campaign.

Human Rights and American Security

A human rights campaign embarked upon by a great power entails large costs. Were this not so, a case might be made for a global commitment to human rights as providing the American people with a moral basis for foreign policy with which to oppose the Communist ideology, whose acknowledged global aim is to eliminate capitalism and "bourgeois democracy." The costs of such a commitment, however, are subtle and readily overlooked. If we are to make human rights the centerpiece of our foreign policy, we cannot limit this to our global rivals. We must condemn as well violations by client regimes that may lack institutions or traditions that protect the human rights of their citizens and may in addition be dangerously threatened by external or internal enemies—a difficult time in which to learn the practice of democracy and liberalism. A South Korea under threat from a militaristic North Korea, for example, ought not to be pressed by the United States to emulate our political institutions or, failing to do so, have to face its mortal enemy in isolation.

In deliberating on the place of human rights in U.S. foreign policy, we must keep in view that our central concern must be to protect U.S. security and to promote a world in which our democratic way of life will be safe. Our capacity to resist the evils of Soviet expansionism and to choose among possible allies the ones that politically are more virtuous, or at least less evil, depends on our geopolitical position in the world. Just as we were forced into an alliance with Stalin in 1941 in order to rectify the balance against Hitler and have found it necessary in the past decade to move toward alliance with a despotic China, so a further weakening of NATO relative to the Soviet Bloc could narrow our discretion in choosing future allies.

Of course, the U.S. government should use its influence to discourage immoral practices by governments that depend on us for assistance, while recognizing the necessary limits of our beneficent influence. (Of course, U.S. leaders need not physically embrace every dictator who stands with us in the cold war, to say nothing of those who stand against us.) To do so does not require us to adopt an ideological foreign policy based on a global commitment to human rights. If the U.S. government has the limited aim of ameliorating the police activities of our less liberal allies, we can do so pragmatically, according to the particular circumstances of the human rights violations that provoke our intervention and of the internal and foreign dangers that imperil the regime. The U.S. government will also have occasion to alert the world to particularly heinous human rights violations by our Communist adversaries, whether it is the expulsion of boat people from Cuba and Vietnam or the Soviet Union's repression of dissident intellectuals. Moreover, the U.S. government can privately intervene with other governments, whether hostile or otherwise, to encourage humane treatment of men and women whose rights are being abused. Indeed, we can manifest our concern that governments respect the human rights of their citizens without proclaiming ideological warfare against our allies, our antagonists, and by logical extension the majority of the world's governments. In a word, we are not obliged to choose between excluding Solzhenitsyn from the White House and launching a worldwide human rights crusade.

The U.S. government after all is not the last resort of human rights victims the world over. One of the strengths of democratic society is the private association whose members pursue common objectives. Western scientists may freely participate in research programs and exchanges with their Soviet peers, or, if they feel revulsion at the repression of admired Soviet intellectuals, they may organize themselves to boycott such exchanges. Newspapers may inform the world of Soviet repression of its citizens and even, within the limits imposed by the regime, help to uncover it. World organizations that are committed to advancing universal human rights may investigate and publicize violations, uniting powerful voices, even including those of Communist parties in democratic countries, in a chorus of condemnation. Why then should the government of the United States launch a campaign on behalf of human rights that cynics will see as self-serving and that indeed *is* obliged to serve the security interests of the people it represents? There will be times when the president of the United States will want to add his voice to that chorus of condemnation, but the less often he is heard campaigning for human rights, the greater will be his power to move public opinion on those extraordinary occasions.

U.S. foreign policy must have a moral foundation if it is to be sustained. That moral foundation cannot be a commitment to universal human rights that disregards the needs of U.S. security. The chief threat to U.S. security emanates from the Soviet-centered Communist movement. Opposition to that movement, to the military machine that is its vehicle and to the totalitarian ideology that drives it, is the real moral equivalent of war.

Notes

1. See David Riesman, "Prospects for Human Rights," *Society*, November–December 1977, pp. 28–33; also Alan Tonelson, "Pitfalls of Morality," *New Republic*, 29 October 1977, pp. 13–15.

2. See Laurie S. Wiseberg and Harry Scoble, "Human Rights and Soviet American Relations," a paper written for the Kenyon Public Affairs Conference Center, 1980, p. 3.

3. Amnesty International and other such organizations may be universalists, seeking out violations of human rights wherever they occur, but their individual members do not appear to be indifferent to the source of the violations.

4. *Public Papers of the Presidents, Jimmy Carter* (Washington, D.C.: U.S. Government Printing Office, 1977), vol. I, p. 2.

5. Ibid., p. 962 (Notre Dame Commencement Address, 22 May 1977).

6. Ibid., pp. 341, 503, 765, and 1107.

7. Ibid., pp. 765–66 (Question and Answer Session with European Broadcast Journalists).

8. Ibid., p. 385 (Question and Answer Session at Clinton, Mass.).

9. Ibid., p. 766 (Question and Answer Session with European Broadcast Journalists).

10. Ibid., p. 499 (President's News Conference, 24 March 1977).

11. Ibid., p. 958 (Notre Dame Commencement Address).

12. Ibid., p. 913 (Question and Answer Session with Area Residents, Los Angeles, 17 May 1977).

13. Ibid., p. 947 (Question and Answer Session with Publishers etc., 20 May 1977).

14. Ibid., p. 958 (Notre Dame Commencement Address).

15. Ibid., p. 1107 (President's News Conference, 13 June 1977).

16. Ibid., p. 541 (Question and Answer Session with Reporters, 30 March 1977).

17. Ibid., p. 947 (Question and Answer Session with Publishers etc.).

18. See Elizabeth Drew, "Human Rights," *New Yorker*, 18 July 1977, pp. 36–62.

19. Notre Dame Commencement Address in *Public Papers of the President*, pp. 956–57.

20. Quoted by Drew, "Human Rights," p. 41.

21. In theory the United States' estimate might diverge from the Soviet estimate in supposing that reduced repression would actually lead to instability, but in practice the USSR is in a far better position than the United States to judge the probable effects of its own policies.

22. President's News Conference, 8 February 1977, in *Public Papers of the President*, p. 100.

23. The only apparent exception is to be found in some nationalist groups in Transcaucasia whose political credentials are suspect.

6

From Helsinki to Madrid

James Ring Adams

The centerpiece of Western human rights efforts in the last half of the 1970s was the so-called Helsinki process, the series of pan-European conferences (including the United States, Canada, and the USSR) initiated by the summit meeting that adopted the Helsinki accords. As this "process" proceeded through follow-up meetings in Belgrade in 1977–78 and Madrid in 1980–83, it was constantly beset by questions about the ultimate worth of the Helsinki accords. Had the West won a subtle but significant victory at the 1975 Helsinki summit and had it held this ground in the follow-up meetings? Or were these sessions futile or worse, revealing Western complacency in the face of blatant violations by the Soviet Union and Eastern Europe? In the light of martial law in Poland, the Soviet invasion of Afghanistan, the constant repression and ultimate disbanding of the Soviet "Helsinki Watch Groups," and an unrepentant pattern of other abuses, should the whole thing be called off?

The answer to these questions depended on the criteria used. By the hardened measures of geopolitics, the largest gainer was the Soviet Union. It won what it considered to be international recognition for its Eastern European dominion and for a rearrangement of German territory that sundered that greatest of European threats and pushed it back from Russian soil. By the more intangible considerations of moral and political principles, and their potential for inspiring political action, the West may have carried the high ground. Intangibles may not count for much in diplomacy if we are at the wrong end of an unfavorable balance of forces. For a lasting illustration, we need only turn to Thucydides' recounting of the Athenians' decision to annihilate the Melians in disregard of the Melians' appeal to justice and religious law. But in a geopolitical stalemate in which neither contender is willing to go to such extremes, the intangibles may come to have substance. The appeal to justice, which at least made the Melians remembered, may also have a practical effect. If the competition between superpowers remains largely at the level of the intangibles, then the Helsinki Final Act may be very useful to the West. Unlike other international human rights documents in their current state of interpretation, it embodies a definition of justice that is squarely in the Western liberal tradition.

It remains to be seen whether Helsinki can be judged a success in terms of the criterion of moral principles. Attitudes toward this "process" vary widely depending on whether observers focus upon displays of Western unity on the issue of human rights or continuing Soviet abuses of human rights. But a decision about the future of the Helsinki process will be more important in the long run to U.S. human rights policy than the sterile debate between Carter and Reagan appointees on distinguishing between "totalitarian" and "authoritarian" dictatorships. That exercise may be useful as a theoretical classification of regimes, but it is no substitute for political prudence in choosing friends, enemies, or countries to leave alone. Older editions of Webster's dictionary illustrate the distinction by citing Nazi Germany as totalitarian and Fascist Italy as authoritarian. Yet the Western liberal democracies fought both countries in the name of human rights while recognizing the neutrality of Fascist Spain and lionizing the heroic contribution of their thoroughly totalitarian ally, the Stalinist USSR. The Helsinki process goes to the core of any official U.S. stance toward human rights because the Helsinki accords are one of the basic international instruments for defining human rights and, in spite of everything, remain the best available for defending the traditional Western meaning of the idea.

It is a major paradox that this should be so. The Helsinki conference was the goal of twenty years of Soviet diplomacy and was accepted only reluctantly by the West. The West, and the United States in particular, had pinned its hopes on the United Nations. Even though the Soviets at first disliked this institution, it is now busily subverting the coherent liberal content of the United Nations' "human rights" declarations. Likewise, the West managed to impose *its* definitions on Helsinki terms. Persistent Western effort was required to bring about this sea change in Helsinki, just as Western inattention had made it easier for the United Nations to deteriorate. But the achievement of the liberal democracies remained tentative and could be easily eclipsed.

The Road to Helsinki

To understand the nature of this sea change, and the worries about its permanence, let us retrace the history of the Helsinki conference. Surprising as it later might seem, the idea of a pan-European summit conference originated with the Soviet Union in the 1954 peace initiative following Stalin's death. Western analysts interpreted the Soviet goal as ratification of the postwar boundaries of Europe, which the Red Army had redrawn to Russia's marked advantage. (Among other adjustments, the Soviets incorporated Immanuel Kant's Konigsberg—now Kaliningrad—not only into the USSR but into the Russian Federated SSR.) The Soviet proposal included a plan for a permanent commission on European security, which would give the USSR a seat among the deliberations of European NATO members while excluding the United States. This proposal was a transparent attempt to extend Soviet influence in Western Europe.

As such, this initiative was virtually ignored by the West until the mid 1960s. Henry Kissinger writes in his memoirs that in the second half of the decade domestic political pressure for such a conference began to grow among NATO allies, partly because of doubts about U.S. steadiness in Europe. On 3 April 1969, Soviet Ambassador Anatoly Dobrynin conveyed to the White House the latest Warsaw Pact call for the conference, adding that the Soviets no longer objected to U.S. participation. In the face of "enormous eagerness within the Alliance," Dr. Kissinger proposed that the United States agree, in principle, provided progress occurred on such concrete European issues as Berlin. He thus succeeded in putting the conference "on a slow track." "But once launched," he writes, "a diplomatic process cannot be controlled simply by formal declarations—especially from the office of the security adviser in the White House basement. . . . Significant policy deviations begin as minor departures whose effect becomes apparent only as they are projected into the future."[1] In the next two years, the Western preconditions were met. In return for a preliminary conference, but not necessarily a summit, the Soviets ratified the 1971 Four-Power Agreement on Berlin and agreed to start Mutual and Balanced Force Reduction Talks on troop levels in central Europe. The United States was left without further excuse for delay. In November 1972 the first preparatory session of the Conference on Security and Cooperation in Europe (CSCE) formally convened in Helsinki.

As preparatory talks later shifted to Geneva, Western delegates could claim a few further advances. Negotiations were grouped in what came to be called "baskets": Basket 1 on security measures; Basket 2 on cooperation in economics, science, and technology; and Basket 3 on humanitarian and other issues. It was Basket 3 that inspired the public to link this conference with human rights. The press began to pay attention to Western European demands for concessions on family reunification, easier contacts between people, freer flow of information, and the like. The Netherlands took a leading role in this effort, prompting TASS to accuse it by name of "hampering" the conference[2] and prompting the U.S. delegation headed by Albert W. Sherer, Jr., to urge "greater realism" on its allies.

While public attention focused on Basket 3, more profound talks were underway on Basket 1. Along with technical details on "confidence-building measures," such as prior notification about certain military maneuvers, the delegates also drafted ten "Principles Guiding Relations Between Participating States." Certain of these primarily served Soviet purposes, such as Principle III, "Inviolability of frontiers," and Principle VI, "Nonintervention in internal affairs." But Principle VII, "Respect for human rights and fundamental freedoms, including the freedom of thought, conscience, religion or belief," was basically a product of the Western liberal tradition.[3] Its true significance began to emerge only after formal adoption of the Helsinki Final Act.

In the meantime, as the CSCE Final Act was signed amid great pomp in Helsinki on 1 August 1975, many observers remained skeptical. The gathering of thirty-five sovereignties was said to be the largest European summit since the Congress of Vienna convened in September 1814; along with President Ford and General Secretary Brezhnev, "High Representatives" attended from Liechtenstein, Monaco, San Marino, and the Holy See. The Helsinki summit was hardly to be compared to the Congress of Vienna in terms of diplomatic potency; the Final Act was not a legally binding treaty. But the analogy to the conference that redrew the boundaries of post-Napoleonic Europe struck a dissonant chord with U.S. public opinion. Some commentators stated that the accords did what the Yalta agreements were said to have done in dividing Europe but actually had not. (The Yalta agreements, in spite of their notoriety, had called for free elections in Eastern Europe.) Much U.S. editorial comment was hostile to the Helsinki summit. The *Wall Street Journal* urged, "Jerry, don't go."[4] President Ford states in his memoirs, "No journey I made during my Presidency was so widely misunderstood." He cites Helsinki as one of the factors that prompted Ronald Reagan to challenge him in the 1976 Republican presidential primaries.[5]

This hostility was a reaction to the spectacle of an international summit endorsing the postwar geopolitical gains of the Soviet Union. The human rights language in the Final Act was largely overlooked. Yet in one of the great political surprises of the decade, this language quickly attained a degree of influence that overshadowed most of the other aspects of the accord. In hindsight, this development may appear understandable. The Helsinki Final Act was designed as a didactic document. It drew its force from the willingness of so many heads of state to agree on a statement of general principles. The Final Act expressly appealed to public opinion. One of its concluding paragraphs called on each participating state to disseminate the full text "and make it known as widely as possible."[6] It was only natural that public opinion would seize on the document's broad moral declarations rather than on its technicalities, such as visas for journalists.

Public Opinion and "Competitive Decadence"

This development was especially striking within the Soviet Union and its East European domain. Official circles in the USSR embraced the Final Act warmly, circulating it by the hundreds of thousands and even incorporating the ten guiding principles into the 1977 Brezhnev Constitution. But unofficial circles quickly grasped its other possibilities. The group of scientists and intellectuals attracted to Andrei Sakharov's

Human Rights Committee had already developed the technique of comparing the Soviet government's deeds to the principles and procedures of its laws. This method of writing appeals to government officials had earned them the sobriquet of *zakonniki,* "the legalists." The Helsinki document gave them a broader set of standards, signed by the Soviet Union, and an international forum for appeal.

In May 1976, Professor Yuri Orlov and ten other Soviet citizens founded the Moscow Helsinki Watch Group. Its first public statement described its agenda.

> The Group considers that its most urgent task is to inform all Heads of State signatory to the Final Act of August 1, 1975, and the public at large of direct violations of the provisions mentioned above.
>   In this regard the group:
>   1) will accept directly from Soviet citizens written complaints which concern them personally and which relate to the (humanitarian) provisions. . . . The Group will forward such complaints in abridged form to all Heads of States signatory to the Final Act and will inform the public at large of the substance of the complaints. The Group will retain the original complaint signed by the author;
>   2) will gather, with the assistance of the public, other information on violations of the provisions mentioned above, organize this information, evaluate its reliability and forward it to Heads of States and to the public.[7]

The Moscow group appealed to "the public of the other participating states" to form their own groups to monitor their own governments. Its lead was followed within the Soviet Union in the Ukraine, Lithuania, Armenia, and Georgia. According to the U.S. Commission on Security and Cooperation in Europe, this example inspired other Soviet rights groups, such as the Christian and Catholic Committees to Defend the Rights of Believers; the Adventist, Pentecostal, and Baptist rights groups; the Working Commission on the Abuse of Psychiatry for Political Purposes; and the Invalids' Rights Group. It was followed outside the USSR by the New York–based Helsinki Watch and the U.S. commission itself, as well as by Charter 77 in Czechoslovakia and by KOR (the Workers' Defense Committee) in Poland.[8]

These groups seized on the crucial paragraph seven of Principle VII: "They (the participating states) confirm the right of the individual to know and act upon his rights and duties in this field." In the view of one authority on international law, this paragraph emphasized the individual's role "in a very original way." The Helsinki summit was unable to follow the lead of the UN International Covenants on Human Rights and set up machinery allowing an aggrieved individual to petition directly to an international body; all decisions of the CSCE require unanimous consent, and the socialist countries would never have agreed.[9] But this paragraph also repudiated the view that individual rights could be deferred in the name of a government's pursuit of "group rights." Furthermore, by its presence in the Final Act, this language emphasized that each of the thirty-five participants could claim a legitimate interest in the human rights of individuals in each other's jurisdictions. By giving this emphasis to the individual's action and by urging that the Final Act be made "known as widely as possible," the Helsinki summit, wittingly or not, had invited unofficial public opinion to take part in the Helsinki process.

Although the appeal to "peace-loving" public opinion has been a frequent theme of the Soviet version of détente, the aftermath of Helsinki turned this appeal in another direction. The Soviet themes of security and disarmament were supplemented with the Western theme of human rights. Helsinki thus took on an intangible but far from negligible role in the struggle that Leopold Labedz has felicitously termed "competitive decadence."[10] As Pierre Hassner described this struggle in a 1973 essay,

> Among blocs, alliances or regional organizations . . . it becomes a matter . . . of comparative resistance to the forces of disintegration which eat away at all of them and which will be encouraged by their mutual acceptance and interpenetration. . . .
>
> Within this complex process (where the Soviet Union is increasingly superior militarily, and the Western countries are superior on the economic and technical level), the most decisive element is in fact the crisis, both social and spiritual, of modern society. This crisis is more visible and diffuse in the West; it is more controlled but more explosive in the East.[11]

The question becomes, which society, East or West, will suffer more from this malaise of modernity. The competition becomes one of maintaining one's own self-confidence and political legitimacy while awaiting the disintegration of the self-confidence and legitimacy of the other. Hassner contended that, at the time of his essay, the Soviet Union appeared more optimistic about the outcome and certainly more lucid about "this new state of fluidity." But he observed at the very beginning of the preparatory talks for Helsinki:

> Rarely have force and diplomacy rested on such implicit gambles about their effects on long-term historical, political and economic, but above all psychological or social processes. . . .
>
> There is thus a two-fold paradox in this current era of negotiation. On the one hand, all this spectacular activity amounts basically to recognizing the status quo. Yet, on the other hand, this recognition of the status quo could activate psychological and social forces that would undermine it far more powerfully, because more unpredictably, than all diplomatic or military undertakings now being contemplated.[12]

The Follow-Up Begins

The gamble of Helsinki, moreover, was not limited to the Final Act. The weight of the Helsinki process subsequently shifted to a provision that, if not quite double or nothing, certainly kept the diplomatic game going. This was Basket 4, the call for a "Follow-up to the Conference."[13] The Final Act explicitly called for a review meeting in Belgrade in 1977 and for at least one more thereafter. Like the Helsinki conference itself, this continuation was originally sought most avidly by the Soviet Union. It was the main point of the first speech at the CSCE in Vienna, delivered on 3 July 1973, by Soviet Foreign Minister Andrei Gromyko. The Final Act compromise denied the Soviets the permanent European security commission they had sought. The West still remained wary of Soviet goals. Furthermore, perhaps mindful of the sorry state of the United Nations, the participants were very reluctant to establish another standing international bureaucracy. They settled instead on a series of periodic review conferences, a feature peculiar to the Helsinki process and one that greatly intensified its impact on the "psychological and social forces" in Europe and the United States.

For the dissidents of the USSR and Eastern Europe, the Belgrade review became the focus of activity. The drafters of Charter 77 in Czechoslovakia gave it that name in large part to connect it to the scheduled date of the Belgrade conference. The Communist bloc ferment on human rights also had an impact on public opinion in the United States. Americans seemed surprised by the vitality of the overseas appeal of their basic political tradition. The rights embodied in the U.S. Constitution were being eagerly sought by people of evident decency and intelligence who had been thoroughly exposed to Communist doctrine and practice. In retrospect, this period marked a watershed from the self-doubt of the Vietnam War. It was marked by the performance of Daniel Patrick Moynihan as U.S. ambassador to the United Nations and his later defeat of the antiwar activist Bella Abzug in the New York Democratic primary for U.S. senator. Human rights emerged in the United States as a major theme in both diplomacy and domestic politics before the election of Jimmy Carter to the presidency. The involvement of public opinion greatly changed the nature of U.S. diplomacy toward the CSCE.

The main institutional expression of this new public involvement was the formation of the U.S. Commission on Security and Cooperation in Europe. This unique body was created by the U.S. Congress in the spring of 1976 on the initiative of Representative Millicent Fenwick (R.–New Jersey). She received the idea during a talk with Soviet dissidents in Moscow. This joint legislative-executive commission is made up of six senators, six representatives, and one official each from the Departments of State, Commerce, and Defense. In spite of reports that Secretary of State Henry Kissinger was reluctant to cooperate, the commission quickly became the dominant sounding board for public concern with Helsinki, both at home and in Europe. It held numerous public hearings and published a variety of reports, including translations of the complete reports of the Moscow Helsinki Watch Group. Following its legislative mandate, it received semiannual reports from the president on the performance of the signers of the Final Act. On the whole, the commission should be counted the most valuable contribution Congress has made to U.S. foreign policy in the recent past. Congress succeeded here where it has failed so often in foreign policy because its unique competence lies in representing the public, and Helsinki diplomacy, unlike the other varieties, rests in the highest sense on the appeal to public opinion.

The formation of the U.S. Commission on Security and Cooperation in Europe greatly broadened the official constituency for the upcoming Belgrade talks. The State Department at first had planned to handle the meeting in the same way it had handled the Helsinki preparatory talks, with career diplomats and a "balanced" approach to the review. But pressure from the commission and the public changed the original intention to send a low-profile delegation headed by a State Department veteran. The delegation was expanded to include public figures and commission members. The assignment of heading it went to former Supreme Court Justice and UN Ambassador Arthur Goldberg, who turned out to be not the worst choice for the job. This broadening of the delegation and the appointment of Ambassador Goldberg came just weeks before the October 4 convening of the conference, however, and irritated professionals long involved in the CSCE. In the words of Harold S. Russell, principal U.S. negotiator of the ten guiding principles, "A small delegation of professional diplomats found itself swamped by literally dozens of congressional and public members who had little knowledge of or interest in the overall context of the negotiations."[14]

Belgrade

These tensions may have contributed to a shaky start at Belgrade, but in the course of the conference Western delegations rallied around their right to question the Soviet and East European performance on human rights. The Soviet Union at first rejected these questions as an intervention in its internal affairs in violation of Principle VI. But U.S. and Western European speakers insisted that, as Ambassador Goldberg stated in his November 3 speech in the Basket 1 working group, "We are all subject to broad international legal obligations concerning human rights, and, in plain language, a state's fulfillment of its international legal obligations is not exclusively its own business." Ambassador Goldberg further argued that the Principle VI language on nonintervention was customarily understood in international law to refer only to interventions involving a use or threat of force—in other words, actions "aimed not at persuasion but at compulsion."[15]

Ambassador Goldberg's speeches produced a turning point in Soviet tactics. Thoroughly irritated, the Soviets retaliated with a speech condemning alleged Western violations of human rights, such as U.S. treatment of the Wilmington ten and the American Indian Movement. Whatever embarrassment this speech may have caused the United States proved easy to manage, because these accusations undercut the Soviet delegation's own earlier insistence that such criticisms were off limits. By attempting to turn the human rights issue against the West, Russian diplomats in effect admitted that it was a legitimate topic for an international forum.

The winning of this point may be said to constitute the main accomplishment of the first session at Belgrade. When the initial session concluded in mid November, Western delegations had maintained a united front on human rights; several speakers from Europe had gone so far as to name the names of the Soviet Helsinki Watch Group members who had been jailed for their monitoring activities; and a commitment had been maintained on holding a second follow-up conference two years later.

When the Belgrade conference reconvened after the December holidays, the West expected the concluding session to work on drafting the final communiqué. Instead, the Soviets laid a brief final draft on the table, incorporating most of the East's criticism of the West and excluding all of the West's criticism of the East. The Soviet delegation insisted in a near ultimatum that this draft stand as the final communiqué. Most delegates at the conference interpreted this stand as an admission of weakness, indicating that the Soviets had failed to gain whatever they sought from the meeting and wanted to wind it down as quickly as possible. The Soviet position unified the NATO and nonaligned groups in opposition and even irritated some of the Warsaw Pact delegations.[16] Subsequent negotiations expanded the Soviet draft somewhat, but the final communiqué pointedly omitted any explicit mention of human rights. Its main feature was to call for a second follow-up conference in Madrid on 11 November 1980, as well as for three interim "experts' meetings."

The outcome produced a heated controversy among two different CSCE constituencies. Some of the most militant human rights advocates, including Soviet dissidents, were bitterly disappointed by the willingness of Helsinki participants to continue meeting while members of the Soviet Helsinki Watch Groups were being jailed for nothing more than promoting observance of the Final Act. Undeterred by the impending Belgrade conference, the Soviet government had arrested nine of the eleven original members of the Moscow Helsinki Watch Group. The group's leader, Yuri Orlov, was one of the first to be jailed, and during the preparatory session in Belgrade Alexander Ginsburg, another member, was convicted of anti-Soviet agitation and propaganda. In Czechoslovakia, the three principal sponsors of Charter 77 had been arrested or interrogated, and one, philosophy professor Jan Patocka, had died a week after an eleven-hour session with police. Vladimir Bukovsky, an exiled Soviet dissident, maintained that his colleagues had hoped the balancing of the three baskets in the Final Act would provide leverage by which states that violated human rights could be punished by suspensions of trade, scientific cooperation, and the like. He concluded that the West's decision at Belgrade to confine itself to diplomatic confrontation rather than to apply sanctions had destroyed the force of the Final Act.[17]

On the other hand, several professional diplomats long involved in the CSCE complained that Ambassador Goldberg's accusatory speeches and press conferences had destroyed prospects at Belgrade for a number of specific agreements. In a singularly undiplomatic article in *Foreign Policy*, Albert Sherer wrote:

> Goldberg's one thought was to protect Carter's credibility on human rights. As he self-righteously hammered away at the cause of Soviet dissidents, reaping encomiums from emigré groups and the president, he progressively alienated friend and foe alike at the conference.[18]

Harold Russell added, "The result has been charitably criticized as a failure; it may in fact have been much worse."[19] Both writers advocated a "compromise" position at the next follow-up in Madrid. "Dropping its sanctimonious attitude that antagonized so many at Belgrade," wrote Mr. Sherer, "the United States should revert to a lower profile and encourage the West European countries to take the lead."[20]

Madrid

The sentiments of Sherer and Russell may have reflected the second thoughts of some West European governments in the immediate aftermath of Belgrade. But as a measure of the rapid evolution in diplomatic as well as public opinion, this advice was never seriously considered in the preparations for Madrid. For head of the preparatory delegation, the Carter White House chose as chairman former Attorney General Griffin Bell and as cochairman Max M. Kampelman, a Washington lawyer and Democratic party policy adviser closely associated with the pro–human rights, anti-Soviet outlook of Senators Daniel Patrick Moynihan and Henry Jackson. After the change in administration, Attorney General Bell resigned and Ambassador Kampelman was elevated to chairman. Instead of the five or so public members on the Belgrade delegation, the Madrid delegation included thirty. The principal measure of confrontation at these meetings had become the naming of persecuted dissidents; it was almost an index of a delegation's "toughness." At Belgrade less than a dozen had been named. Speakers at Madrid mentioned over one hundred.

Some professional diplomats attributed this posture to President Carter's campaign for reelection. The public representation was broadened, they said, to placate crucial domestic constituencies. Other delegations at Madrid may have tended to discount U.S. rhetoric. But the international situation had also changed, and developments since Belgrade had seriously undercut the advocates of a low-profile approach. First came the Soviet invasion of Afghanistan in December 1979, which weakened remaining illusions about the value of detente. Next to the U.S. partial grain embargo and Olympic boycott, the rhetoric at Belgrade seemed mild, and the issue before the West at Madrid was less how to restore harmony to the CSCE than whether to continue the process at all. Second was the success of the Belgrade approach at the Scientific Forum in Hamburg, one of the experts' meetings provided for in the Belgrade communiqué. The two-week-long meeting convened in February 1980 with the memory of Afghanistan and the internal exile of Nobel laureate Andrei Sakharov fresh in the delegates' minds. The denunciations of the Soviet Union exceeded in intensity anything heard at Belgrade, yet the Soviet delegation sat and took it and then accepted a final communiqué with a specific reaffirmation of human rights.

But the most influential development of the time was the apparent regeneration of Poland. Historians may debate forever how directly the Polish workers' upheaval and the unprecedented concessions demanded and temporarily won by Solidarity were influenced by the Helsinki process. Some links may be drawn through the Helsinki Watch Groups and KOR, the Polish dissident intellectuals' Workers' Defense Committee (later KSS, for Committee for Social Self-Defense). Yet the influence of purely Polish history—the workers' riots in Gdansk in 1970 and in Radom and Ursus in 1976, the election of Karol Cardinal Wojtyla as pope—was so powerful that external influences may have been marginal at best. It may fairly be said, however, that Poland confirmed Pierre Hassner's vision of the unleashing of "psychological and social forces" more powerful and more unpredictable "than all diplomatic or military undertakings now being contemplated."

Now more than ever before in the Helsinki process, the Madrid conference felt itself to be a sideshow. From the beginning of the formal meetings delegates were well aware that nothing they did could have as much importance for the future of Europe as events 1,500 miles away on the opposite corner of the continent. They tacitly recognized (or feared) that their tedious negotiations could be obliterated in an instant by the stampede from the center ring if anything went wrong with the Polish attempt at lion- (or should we say, bear-) taming.

Polish events played little direct role in the first two phases of Madrid (11 November–18 December 1980 and 27 January–28 July 1981). There were subterranean currents. Some Polish diplomats raised eyebrows by stating that their countrymen would fight a Soviet invasion. One report circulated that the Soviets were excluding the Poles from some of the inner Warsaw Pact caucuses. The Eastern bloc seemed more loosely coordinated than at Belgrade or Helsinki. But the Madrid agenda had little to do with the rise of Solidarity and the disarray in the Polish Communist party.

The main new initiative at the conference was the call for yet more conferences. Most of the wrangling centered on the proposal for a post-Madrid Conference on Disarmament in Europe (CDE, in the alphabetic jargon of the CSCE). A French proposal endorsed by NATO would have focused the CDE on new "confidence and security-building measures" (again alphabetized, in a distillation of diplomatic jargon, to CSBMs). The most prominent CSBM in the Final Act required advance notification of military maneuvers exceeding 25,000 troops that take place on European territory (or in the case of the USSR and Turkey, within 250 miles of their European borders).[21] The French proposal would have extended this scope from the Atlantic to the Urals. Since this area included all of the European USSR, the West was startled when, in a February 23 speech to the 26th Congress of the CPSU, Leonid Brezhnev accepted the idea. He insisted, however, that NATO make a "corresponding move"; Soviet negotiators subsequently defined "corresponding" to mean inclusion of North American territory. While the neutral/nonaligned contingent (ranging from Sweden to San Marino) labored to find an intermediate formula, the NATO caucus negotiated on ground rules for the security forum. The purpose of the Western alliance was to keep this future meeting from becoming a one-sided sounding board for Soviet propaganda. (That the security forum rhetoric might cut two ways became apparent, however, when U.S. Ambassador Kampelman defined the purpose of the meeting as the reducing of the risk of surprise attack. A surprise attack on Europe is likely from only one quarter.)[22]

The West also insisted on pairing the CDE with post-Madrid experts' meetings on human rights and family reunification. Other outstanding issues included insertion of strong human rights language in the final communiqué and further progress on Basket 3. A slew of agreements had been reached on minor new proposals by the middle of phase two, but the few areas of disagreement were the big ones. The summer session dragged on and on. The main point of consensus was that no one wanted to spend August in Madrid. A late July flurry of activity tried to wrap up the conference with a global compromise and a substantive communiqué. But the effort petered out as the Soviets hardened their position. The conference recessed until October 27.

The Polish Coup

In the interval the center ring performance in Poland grew more and more dramatic. Solidarity went from strength to strength; the native Communist rulers lost their grip and their nerve; and ominously, through yet unrevealed maneuvering, leadership in the Politburo was handed to an army general. Oblivious to the gathering tension, the delegates reconvened for the fall session and droned on. In fairness to the CSCE, it should be noted that the West in general missed the warning signs. Planning had concentrated on the awesome possibility of a full-scale Russian invasion of Poland. Very few seemed to know what to do about a homegrown coup d'etat that suppressed Solidarity to Soviet satisfaction but also supplanted the forms of Communist rule. Washington itself hesitated before identifying the coup as a sophisticated form of Soviet intervention, carefully prepared and executed with the aid of the Red Army. Even so, the delayed reaction at Madrid to the Polish martial law contrasts pitifully with the hopes in the summer session that the CSCE might help deter direct Soviet intervention. So completely did the Soviets and their Polish agents disregard the CSCE that the crackdown came just days before the scheduled adjournment of the conference. Just two days before the coup, in fact, the neutral/nonaligned delegates had submitted a draft final communiqué. It was being discussed as a possible compromise even as martial law clamped down on Poland. Further CSCE negotiations seemed pointless after this intrusion of reality, and so on December 18 the delegates recessed again in some confusion.

On 9 February 1982, Western delegations arrived for the fourth phase of the conference with a clearer strategy and a largely unified front. An imposing array of foreign ministers flew in for the express purpose of denouncing events in Poland, but negotiations on CSCE business were suspended. There were some nuances of attitude within the NATO caucus. Ambassador Kampelman arrived with a delegation from which the professional negotiators had been purposely deleted. West Germany, which had raised eyebrows throughout Europe by its mild reaction to the Polish crackdown, wanted to remain open to negotiating possibilities during the session. But any divergent tendencies within the West were quickly squelched by the remarkable events of the opening day, Tuesday, February 9.

By the quirks of the Helsinki process the chairman was the Polish delegate, Wlodzimierz Konarski. With a room full of foreign ministers waiting to speak, he stalled and hampered the proceedings with a series of highly questionable procedural rulings. At the end of the allotted time, he attempted to close the meeting practically in the face of French Foreign Minister Claude Cheysson. After a seven-hour procedural struggle, Mr. Cheysson's speech was finally delayed three days, to Friday. This heavy-handed use of the gavel, supported mainly by the Soviet Union, did wonders to unify the West. The fourth phase of Madrid closed five weeks later, having been preoccupied with little else but Poland and human rights.[23]

Still, all this rhetoric made no apparent impact on Poland or the Soviet Union. Polish martial law continued unabated, even though it violated the basic provisions of the Final Act. The Soviet occupation of Afghanistan ground on, in violation of most if not all of the ten guiding principles. The KGB intensified its prosecution of dissidents. On 6 September 1982, the KGB campaign produced its most striking success; in a turning point in the history of Soviet dissidence, the Moscow Helsinki Watch Group decided to disband. Arrests and exiles had whittled the group to three active members, all women (whom the Soviet authorities treated somewhat less harshly then men) or pensioners and including the wife of Andrei Sakharov, who was under severe pressure in her own right. On the day the authorities brought criminal charges against Sofia Kalistratova, a Moscow defense lawyer who was one of these three, the group issued its 195th and final document. After listing sixteen members currently in jail, labor camp, or internal exile, noting the arrests of nearly all the members of the groups in Armenia, Georgia, Lithuania, and the Ukraine, and reporting the charges against Kalistratova, this bulletin concluded, "the Group cannot fulfill the responsibilities which it assumed, and under pressure from the authorities, it is forced to end its activities."[24]

During the fifth phase of the Madrid meeting, the question emerged with greater force than ever before whether the Helsinki process was worth it. Even some of its more constant supporters began to speak of its stagnation. Barring another incident like the insult to M. Cheysson, Western unity seemed to be wavering. When added to the doubts surrounding the original Helsinki summit, the balance sheet might seem decidedly negative.

Human Rights: The Helsinki Declaration vs. the United Nations

Yet such an analysis gives too little weight to the intangible assets for the West in the Helsinki Final Act. As long as the preservation of a political-military balance enables intangibles to remain important, the Helsinki process offers one crucial advantage to the West. The theory of human rights embedded in the Final Act is primarily that of the Western liberal tradition. To understand the importance of this fact, one must understand how international legal standards of human rights have evolved during the postwar era. Taking United Nations declarations as the crucial documents, Dr. Antonio Cassese, professor of international law and director of the Post-Graduate School of International Affairs of the University of Florence, identifies three postwar phases of concern with human rights. The first was that of the Universal Declaration of Human Rights (1945–60), substantially adopting "the Western model of relations between State and individual," emphasizing civil and political rights, and specifically including the right to property. The second phase (1960–73) attempted to turn the moral standards into legal documents, with some provisions for implementation, but it also reflected the growing influence in the United Nations of the Third and socialist worlds. Accordingly, attention turned increasingly to "economic and social rights." In the third phase (1974 to the present), the Third World gained predominance and insisted that "the proclamation of civil and political rights remains a dead letter as long as economic, social and cultural rights are not fully implemented." The Helsinki declaration, writes Dr. Cassese, reflects the second stage of UN developments, with many ideas reminiscent of the first. Because the Helsinki summit was confined to Europe, with very little Third World contribution, and because most of the socialist concessions were in the area of human rights, "the contention seems warranted that the Declaration adopted a Western reinterpretation of UN principles."[25]

To understand how unusual it is to encounter such a document in international forums, one has only to look at the extent to which the United Nations' third phase has perverted any theoretically consistent understanding of human rights. The epitome of this phase was UN General Assembly resolution 32/130, introduced in 1977 by Argentina, Cuba, Iran, the Philippines, and Yugoslavia, an ecumenical coalition of countries sensitive to criticism of their human rights records. This resolution was entitled "Alternative approaches and ways and means within the United Nations system for improving the effective enjoyment of human rights and fundamental freedoms." It redefined human rights to render irrelevant the liberal Western tradition of civil and political rights derived from a social compact. The resolution stated that any judgment on a country's observance of civil and political rights had to take into account whether it also enjoyed "economic, social and cultural rights": "the achievement of lasting progress in the implementation of human rights is dependent upon sound and effective national and international policies of economic and social development." In short, any developing country could defend itself against charges of human rights violations by replying that it hadn't received adequate foreign aid. Resolution 32/130 replaced the ringing phrases of the French Declaration of the Rights of Man and Citizen, as well as the UN Universal Declaration of Human Rights, with the following agenda:

> The international community should accord, or continue to accord, priority to the search for solutions to the mass and flagrant violations of human rights of peoples and persons affected by situations such as those resulting from apartheid, from all forms of racial discrimination, from colonialism, from foreign domination and occupation, from aggression and threats against national sovereignty, national unity and territorial integrity, as well as from the refusal to recognize the fundamental rights of peoples to self-determination and of every nation to the exercise of full sovereignty over its wealth and natural resources.[26]

The resolution also emphasized the priority of "realization of the new international economic order." The measure passed on 16 December 1977, by a vote of 123 to 0 with 15 abstentions including the United States.

This resolution was widely regarded as a transparent attempt to deflect any effective UN criticism of human rights violations. Yet it now stands as international dogma. Furthermore, it is the logical culmination of a confused approach to human rights that can be traced back to the Universal Declaration itself. The Universal Declaration begins with a series of theoretically coherent rights, including the right to own property, but culminates with matters that are less rights than programs of the welfare state, such as unemployment insurance and paid vacations. This confusion is compounded in the United Nations' two International Covenants on Human Rights. The Covenant on Civil and Political Rights, although for the most part traditional, already begins to lose focus in a welter of detail and exceptions, and the "rights of peoples" begin to creep in, diluting the priority of the individual. Furthermore, the right to own property has disappeared.

The problems of this covenant pale in comparison to those of the Covenant on Economic, Social, and Cultural Rights. Yet the second covenant has proved more popular than the first. As Maurice Cranston lucidly explains in *What Are Human Rights?*, "the rights it names are not universal human rights at all."[27] The covenant calls for a number of worthy programs, in education, health, nutrition, and trade unionism, but by elevating them to the status of human rights, it stretches the notion of right beyond coherence. In particular, it states the "right . . . to an adequate standard of living . . . including adequate food, clothing and housing, and to the continuous improvement of living conditions." Since "adequate" is nowhere defined, this provision is as unlimited as human desire. In the United States, for instance, "adequate housing" is generally defined by interior plumbing. If the developing world must meet this standard before it may fairly be asked to pay attention to civil and political rights, as the UN General Assembly now maintains, we reach the absurd conclusion that tent-dwelling nomads who may have treasured the rudiments of political liberty for centuries have no business insisting on their traditional freedom. As Mr. Cranston writes about the first step in this postwar sequence of confusion,

> The effect of a Universal Declaration which is overloaded with affirmations of so-called human rights which are not human rights at all is to push all talk of human rights out of the clear realm of the morally compelling into the twilight world of utopian aspiration.[28]

The Value of Helsinki

For a more extended discussion of the difference between genuine human rights and a program of social legislation, we must refer the reader to Mr. Cranston's perceptive book, as well as to the essay by Clifford Orwin and Thomas Pangle in this collection. Our primary concern here is to evaluate the worth of the Helsinki process. Its greatest value lies in its capacity to rally Western diplomacy to a standard of human rights relatively uncontaminated by the corrupted language of the United Nations. The Helsinki Final Act can be, indeed has been, an immensely valuable didactic document. The need of the West is to see clearly what it says that the United Nations has stopped saying. This clarity was not always to be found in the Carter administration. Not only did President Carter sign the Covenant on Economic, Social, and Cultural Rights, he even coined a new pseudo-right himself. In speaking to the World Health Organization in May 1977, he invented "the right to be free from unnecessary disease."

The Reagan administration has been tempted to err in the opposite direction. In its justifiable impatience with the United Nations' newspeak, it briefly contemplated eliminating the term "human rights" entirely from its official usage, replacing it with the more philosophically coherent term "natural rights." Such a course, however, would have abandoned prematurely the attempt to salvage what remained of the integrity of the international tradition of human rights, an attempt that could center on the Helsinki Final Act.

The Helsinki document may be used to reaffirm fundamental U.S. principles and to spread them to a receptive audience in the East, but only if U.S. participants take every opportunity to preserve their interpretation of its meaning. Fortunately, the requisite rhetoric has not been entirely lacking. U.S. delegations to future sessions could do worse than to evoke the ideas of John Locke and the Declaration of Independence that echo in President Ford's address to the 1975 Helsinki summit:

> Almost 200 years ago the United States of America was born as a free and independent Nation. The descendants of Europeans who proclaimed their independence in America expressed in that declaration a decent respect for the opinions of mankind and asserted not only that all men are created equal, but that they are endowed with inalienable rights to life, liberty, and the pursuit of happiness. The founders of my country did not merely say that all Americans should have these rights, but all men everywhere should have these rights, and these principles have guided the United States of America throughout its two centuries of nationhood. They have given hopes to millions in Europe and on every continent. ... Those principles, though they are still being perfected, remain the guiding lights of American policy and the American people are still dedicated, as they were then, to a decent respect for the opinions of mankind and to life, liberty, and the pursuit of happiness for all peoples everywhere.[29]

These ideas remain powerful even in the face of the extreme disappointment of the Polish people. Fatal as that event might seem for the Helsinki process, it was Poland, not the West, that was changed by the experience. The military seizure of the government—"Bonapartism," Lenin might have called it—swept away the facade of the Polish United Workers Party as well as the formal organization of Solidarity. Communism in Poland may have less popular support than southern Republicanism under military reconstruction and, if the military presence were somehow to be withdrawn, would probably have the same political future. The Helsinki Final Act inaugurated a struggle of ideas that has not yet run its course. The Communist use of force dealt a setback to Western ideals, but at incalculable damage to its own intellectual and moral standing. The question of the ultimate worth of Helsinki remains open, to be answered only by history.

Notes

1. Henry Kissinger, *The White House Years* (Boston: Little, Brown & Co., 1979), pp. 412–16.
2. "Moscow TASS in English," 2105 GMT, 2 March 1974, Foreign Broadcast Information Service, USSR International Affairs, CSCE/RBFR, 4 March 1974.
3. The full text appears in the *Vanderbilt Journal of Transnational Law* 13, nos. 2–3 (Spring–Summer 1980): Appendix A, 575–642. Principle VII reads:

> VII. Respect for human rights and fundamental freedoms, including the freedom of thought, conscience, religion, and belief.
>
> The participating States will respect human rights and fundamental freedoms, including the freedom of thought, conscience, religion or belief, for all without distinction as to race, sex, language or religion.
>
> They will promote and encourage the effective exercise of civil, political, economic, social, cultural and other rights and freedoms, all of which derive from the inherent dignity of the human person and are essential for his free and full development.
>
> Within this framework the participating States will recognize and respect the freedom of the individual to profess and practise, alone or in community with others, religion or belief acting in accordance with the dictates of his own conscience.
>
> The participating States on whose territory national minorities exist will respect the right of persons belonging to such minorities to equality before the law, will afford them the full opportunity for the actual enjoyment of human rights and fundamental freedoms and will, in this manner, protect their legitimate interests in this sphere.
>
> The participating States recognize the universal significance of human rights and fundamental freedoms, respect for which is an essential factor for the peace, justice and well-being necessary to ensure the development of friendly relations and co-operation among themselves as among all States.
>
> They will constantly respect these rights and freedoms in their mutual relations and will endeavour jointly and separately, including in co-operation with the United Nations, to promote universal and effective respect for them.
>
> They confirm the right of the individual to know and act upon his rights and duties in this field.
>
> In the field of human rights and fundamental freedoms, the participating States will act in conformity with the purposes and principles of the Charter of the United Nations and with the Universal Declaration of Human Rights. They will also fulfill their obligations as set forth in the international declarations and agreements in this field including inter alia the International Covenants on Human Rights, by which they may be bound.

4. *Wall Street Journal*, 23 July 1975, p. 14.
5. Gerald A. Ford, *A Time to Heal* (New York: Berkeley Books, 1980), pp. 287, 291.

6. Helsinki Final Act, Basket 4, section 4, paragraph 3; in U.S., Department of State, Bureau of Public Affairs, Office of Media Services, "Conference on Security and Cooperation in Europe, Final Act" (Department of State Publication 8826, General Foreign Policy Series 298/August 1975).

7. Quoted in *Human Rights, International Law and the Helsinki Accord*, ed. Thomas Buergenthal (Montclair, N.J.: Allanheld, Osmun/Universe Books, 1977), p. 121. Some 200 Moscow Helsinki Watch Group reports have been published in English by the U.S. Commission on Security and Cooperation in Europe, Washington, D.C. 20515.

8. "Today the Moscow Helsinki Group Celebrates its Fifth Anniversary," press release of the U.S. Commission on Security and Cooperation in Europe, 12 May 1981. (Although inspired by Helsinki, Charter 77 relies primarily on the International Covenants on Human Rights. KOR, the Workers' Defense Committee, was also, and perhaps primarily, a response to local Polish conditions.)

9. Antonio Cassese, "The Approach of the Helsinki Declaration to Human Rights," *Vanderbilt Journal of Transnational Law* 13, nos. 2–3 (Spring–Summer 1980), p. 286.

10. Quoted by Pierre Hassner in "Europe in the Age of Negotiation," Washington Papers 1, no. 8 (Beverly Hills, Calif.: Sage Publications, 1973).

11. Ibid., pp. 69, 70.

12. Ibid., p. 68.

13. Department of State, "Conference on Security and Cooperation," p. 133.

14. Harold S. Russell, "Follow-up at Madrid: Another Chance for the U.S.," *Vanderbilt Journal of Transnational Law* 13, nos. 2–3 (Spring–Summer 1980), p. 364.

15. Speech of Ambassador Arthur Goldberg, 3 November 1977, "Principle VII: The Intervention Objection and the National Laws and Regulation Defense," distributed by the U.S. CSCE.

16. This version of the conference, derived from Helsinki Watch and CSCE sources, contrasts remarkably with Albert Sherer's insistence that Ambassador Goldberg's performance presented "a golden opportunity . . . for the Soviets to drive wedges within the Western Alliance and between it and the neutral states." See Albert W. Sherer, Jr., "Goldberg's Variations," *Foreign Policy* 39 (Summer 1980): 157. Mr. Sherer accuses Ambassador Goldberg of self-righteousness on the basis of the same speeches that caused some in the United States to accuse him of self-flagellation. Still, there were some glorious moments of rhetoric. Soviet Ambassador Yuli Vorontsov labeled one of former Justice Goldberg's speeches "crude, provocative and pseudo-judicial." Ambassador Goldberg replied in plenary session by quoting Adlai Stevenson's remark to a political opponent: "If you will stop telling lies about me, I'll stop telling the truth about you" (Speech of 11 November 1977).

17. Vladimir Bukovsky, 6 February 1981 interview with National Public Radio, summarized in *CSCE Digest* (newsletter published by the U.S. CSCE), 20 March 1981.

18. Sherer, "Goldberg," pp. 156–57.

19. Russell, "Follow-up at Madrid," p. 365.

20. Sherer, "Goldberg," p. 159.

21. Turkey won a further exemption for territory also contiguous to frontiers shared with "a non-European, non-participating state," i.e., Syria. This particular territory was the staging area for its invasion of Cyprus.

22. Remarks by Ambassador Max M. Kampelman in plenary session, 19 May 1981, in *CSCE Digest*, 29 May 1981, pp. 16–17.

23. See various numbers of *CSCE Digest*, speeches by Ambassador Kampelman.

24. Helsinki Group Document 195 (6 September 1982), translated and reprinted in *A Chronicle of Human Rights in the USSR* 47 (New York: Khronike Press, July–September 1982): 30.

25. Cassese, "Approach," pp. 275–92, especially pp. 276–82.

26. UN General Assembly Resolution 32/130 (16 December 1977).

27. Maurice Cranston, *What Are Human Rights?* (New York: Taplinger Publishing Co., 1973), p. 66.

28. Ibid., p. 68.

29. Gerald Ford, Address at the Conference on Security and Cooperation in Europe, at Finlandia Hall, 1 August 1975; news release of the Department of State, 1 August 1975, Helsinki, Finland, p. 3. The account of the U.S. political tradition in this speech was supplied by Robert A. Goldwin, a special consultant to President Ford and an authority on John Locke and the Declaration of Independence.

7

Human Rights Policy in a Nonliberal World

Carnes Lord

Early in the Carter administration a U.S. official remarked privately that "human rights is the most complicated foreign policy question before the government. No one knows what the policy is, yet it pervades everything we do."[1] By now, the complications of human rights as an aspect and instrument of U.S. foreign policy have become evident to all. Some critics of the Carter administration's record in this area have come to despair of the very possibility of a human rights policy that does not damage U.S. strategic interests by penalizing allies or disrupting relationships with important adversaries. Others have questioned whether a human rights policy grounded in conceptions that are peculiar to Western liberalism can or should form part of U.S. strategy toward the mostly nonliberal Third World.

At the same time, however, it is generally admitted that the idea of human rights has proven, even in its most inchoate versions, an extremely powerful one, with wide popular appeal internationally as well as to the people of the United States. Under these circumstances, an effective human rights policy remains something very much to be desired. Yet it should also be clear that the U.S. commitment to promote human rights around the globe cannot be (as President Carter once put it) "absolute" in the sense that it supersedes every other foreign policy concern. Indeed, if the pursuit of human rights will necessarily obstruct the achievement of fundamental foreign policy goals such as the stability of our alliance relationships, it is not self-evident that the United States should have a human rights policy of any sort.

Essential Requirements of Human Rights Policy

What are the essential requirements of a human rights posture that would be consonant with the fundamental goals of U.S. foreign policy?

125

The first such requirement would seem to be consistency and simplicity. Although any attempt to find a single formula that could be applied in legalistic fashion would clearly be misguided, a policy that defines itself in response to individual cases is no policy at all. There must be certain general principles capable of being readily understood by foreign governments and peoples alike, as well as by the American public. Without such principles, our human rights efforts are likely to appear as capricious and partisan interventions in the affairs of particular states and will be bound to cause resentment even among the populations who are the intended beneficiaries.

A second (and related) requirement is universality. A human rights policy worthy of the name must be capable of application to all countries. Exemptions cannot be allowed routinely in the name of strategic necessity or of the exigencies of development. If the treatment of individual Soviet dissidents is to be regularly protested, the treatment of, say, South Korean dissidents should also be protested and vice versa. Invidious distinctions between countries weaken the force of the entire policy by making it appear opportunistic and politically motivated.

A third requirement of a satisfactory human rights policy is that its primary effect should not be to harm our allies or help our adversaries. If the effect of such a policy is necessarily to destablize allied regimes of authoritarian cast and replace them with authoritarian regimes hostile to the United States or even with weak democratic regimes that invite subversion by the domestic or international Left, its utility must be held highly doubtful. By the same token, allied or friendly states should not be made to bear the brunt of our intervention on behalf of human rights simply because we happen to have greater leverage against them than against adversaries.

Fourth, a human rights policy should help rather than hinder our efforts to extend U.S. influence and win friends among neutral and nonaligned nations. What would seem to be needed generally is a policy that avoids both an intransigently antagonistic posture toward authoritarian Third World regimes (whether of the Right or the Left) and a supine acceptance of the disregard of fundamental human rights by such regimes in the name of security or development. To hew to the first extreme—the course that has been urged in particular by Senator Daniel P. Moynihan—is to push the Third World willy-nilly into the arms of the Russians. To accept the argument that economic development justifies the disregard of fundamental human rights (as was done by the Carter administration or by influential elements within it) is to deprive the United States of the very possibility of principled opposition not only to the excesses of Third World authoritarianism of every stripe but to Soviet communism itself.

A fifth requirement concerns public opinion in the United States. A human rights policy responds to the need evidently felt by many Americans for a foreign policy embodying American ideals as well as

American interests. Yet a number of human rights issues—abortion, affirmative action, and so on—figure prominently in domestic political disputes in this country, and the possibility therefore cannot be excluded that a human rights policy that is improperly conceived or applied will not only lack essential domestic support but could even fuel political quarrels at home. More generally, a human rights policy ought to be designed in such a way as to minimize the tendency of U.S. public opinion to view the rest of the world in moralistic and excessively ideological terms. A human rights policy may become a double-edged weapon if its effect is to make U.S. foreign policy as a whole hostage to the temporary enthusiasms of a domestic public and the selective indignation that has frequently marked media and congressional attention to this issue.

Can these varied and, in part, conflicting requirements be satisfactorily reconciled? I believe they can, but only on the basis of a thorough and fundamental rethinking of the meaning of human rights as an idea and its relationship to the political and cultural systems of the non-Western or nonliberal world. To attempt an adequate theoretical analysis of the idea of human rights is not possible here.[2] I shall merely try to sketch the direction such a rethinking ought to take—a direction corresponding in large measure, though not entirely, to the shifts in human rights policy that have occurred during the Reagan administration.

Human Rights and the Third World

One of the essential purposes of any human rights policy is to make known to the world that the United States stands for something beyond mere material prosperity and offers a model of a kind of society that can satisfy universal human aspirations for freedom and justice. The U.S. pursuit of human rights is exposed in the first instance to the objection that, although perhaps demonstrating that the United States is capable of pursuing some sort of ideal, it holds up an ideal that is unappealing or irrelevant to the concerns of much of contemporary humanity. According to this argument, human rights and the understanding of freedom and justice that they rest on represent a specifically liberal or capitalist ideal that is largely alien to the political culture and irrelevant to the economic and social needs of non-Western peoples.[3]

That there is something to this position has to be frankly acknowledged. It is true that the most authoritative document on the subject of human rights, the Universal Declaration of Human Rights of 1948, was adopted in the United Nations without a dissenting voice, and that nearly all nations continue to give formal acknowledgement to the principles of human rights as formulated in this and subsequent international legal documents and declarations. It is too often forgotten, however, that the Universal Declaration was not unanimously adopted by the countries represented in the United Nations at the time (not only the Soviet bloc but South Africa and Saudi Arabia abstained); and there is good reason to doubt that the new states of the Third World would now ratify the document, at least in its present form, if given the opportunity to do so. The fact is that the Universal Declaration is plainly a Western document in a number of crucial respects. It calls for freedom of conscience or religion and freedom of expression; it includes a right to own property and a right to work and to free choice of employment; above all, it recognizes popular sovereignty and a right to political participation in the form of free elections based on universal and equal suffrage. Not only are these principles not acted on in the great majority of non-Western societies today; in many cases they do not serve even as a model or ideal. And this is so not only for regimes of the Left (or what may perhaps be better described as antitraditional authoritarian regimes oriented toward the Soviet Union), but also for regimes with a traditionalist basis, such as Saudi Arabia, and even for some with a Western orientation and a large measure of free enterprise and constitutional government, such as Singapore or Taiwan. In the nonliberal societies that prevail in the Third World, the very idea of "rights" is an alien importation that remains in some degree suspect. To the extent that rights are understood in the liberal sense as claims of individuals against the community and as essentially prior to the duties required of individuals by the community, they tend to be regarded as corrosive of fundamental social and political bonds. Governments and political leaders tend to view the notion of rights—much as they view the Marxist notion of class struggle—as disruptive of national loyalties and a challenge to the basis of their authority. For the mass of the people, on the other hand, the individualism implicit in the liberal notion of rights often appears destructive of traditional forms of community such as family, tribe, and religion. This is not to say that a certain rhetoric of rights has not come to be employed rather widely in the Third World. But it is characteristic of this rhetoric that it emphasizes the rights of groups above those of individuals. The liberal view of states or of groups or communities generally as voluntary associations of autonomous individuals is a view that remains largely confined to nations with a European cultural heritage.

The weakness of human rights in the Third World has both political and cultural causes. Many Third World states have only recently emerged from colonial status and suffer from severe problems of political integration. In many cases liberal constitutions bequeathed by the departing colonial power were swept away by military juntas or strongmen intent on consolidating central authority in the face of regional, tribal, or factional dissension; and the single party has become the typical political instrument for creating and maintaining loyalty to that authority. Central economic planning has tended to be preferred to free-enterprise capitalism in part for similar reasons and in part in response to a variety of ideological and cultural pressures. Daniel P. Moynihan has argued that the popularity throughout the Third World of soft versions of socialism emphasizing redistribution over production should be traced to the influence of Fabian socialism, promulgated to Third World elites by way of such institutions as the London School of Economics.[4] One wonders whether at least equal importance should not be attributed to the influence of indigenous, precapitalist modes of thought. Notions of redistribution are prominent in the political economy of many primitive societies, and the promotion of "socialist" cooperation over "capitalist" competition is likely to find a congenial reception in a variety of societies with strong tribal or religious traditions.

The Limits to Modernization

Liberal thought has always incorporated certain assumptions concerning what has come to be called political development. For some time, the prevailing assumption was that global economic modernization would lead to the breakdown of traditional societies—societies with autocratic or hierarchical political structures supported by religion—and their transformation into liberal and democratic societies, with liberal political institutions the inevitable byproduct of internal economic development and the growth of a liberal or bourgeois political culture.[5] It is safe to say that this assumption is today increasingly doubted. Those who argued only a few years ago that the growth of a modern economy would encourage political liberalization in the Soviet Union seem to have fallen silent. As for the Third World, although there have been a number of examples of spectacular economic development, there is as yet no unambiguous evidence supporting the proposition that such development will terminate in liberal democracy. In economically successful Asian nations such as Singapore, Taiwan, or South Korea, authoritarian and liberal tendencies coexist in an uneasy accommodation that seems on its way to becoming a permanent feature of the political systems of these countries. In Latin America, prosperity appears at least as likely to issue in political crisis and collapse (Argentina, Chile) as in progress toward democratic stability (Venezuela). Nor is the example of Japan compelling. Although now habitually counted as part of the West, it needs to be remembered that Japan's initial experiment with parliamentary government was not a successful one and that its present liberal constitution was imposed by force of arms. Japan's social and economic practices, which are distinguished by rigidly hierarchical organization and an emphasis on cooperation and solidarity, raise the question whether the postwar transformation of its political culture is as far-reaching or irreversible as is generally assumed. The examples of Japan, India, Nigeria, and a variety of Latin American countries show that liberal political institutions may come into existence under certain conditions in societies that retain strongly preliberal or nonliberal characteristics. Although it is of course necessary that this possibility be thoroughly appreciated in any assessment of the likely impact of a U.S. human rights policy, it is equally important that such a policy not rest on an unwarranted optimism concerning the prospects for transformations of this kind.

The overthrow of the shah of Iran by a popular movement dominated by the Shi'ite clergy offers a further lesson. Although the shah almost certainly acted imprudently in forcing the pace of modernization to the degree he did, the fact remains that the strength of the opposition to him seems to have reflected a considerable measure of popular opposition to any modernization. The United States, which had always regarded its support for the shah as a progressive policy benefiting the mass of the people at the expense of the landed aristocracy and the clergy, suddenly found itself the target of intense popular hostility as the leading champion of atheism, materialism, and moral corruption. The emergence of the Ayatollah Khomeini at the head of the revolution and the new regime only called wide attention to a development that had been under way for some time—the resurgence of Islam as a moral and political force in the Third World. Although it is clearly too soon to assess adequately the implications of this development or to make predictions about the future, its importance can hardly be overestimated. Taken together with evidence that points to the increasing strength of religion within the Communist world (Poland is only the most conspicuous case), not to speak of the recent political explosion of fundamentalist Protestantism in the United States, such developments may portend a radical alteration in the character of world politics in the coming decade and beyond.

Accustomed as they are to taking for granted the separation of church and state as a first principle of political life, Americans have been slow to appreciate the seriousness of the challenge that religion can pose to the liberal outlook. Liberalism in its original form recognized as self-evident truth the idea that men are created equal and endowed with certain inalienable rights. In doing so, it implicitly denied that there are self-evident truths affecting political obligations that derive immediately from divine revelation.[6] The separation of church and state in liberal society presupposes an accommodation of the claims of these institutions that decisively favors the state: The civil authority will abstain from interfering in the religious realm if religion abandons all claim to secular governance. Under the liberal solution, religion, and with it morality generally, becomes an essentially private concern.

It is hardly necessary to say that this sort of solution is very far from being acceptable to all governments—or to all religions—today. In Islam, the Qur'an (Koran) and the law (*shari'a*) deriving from it and from the traditions of the Prophet are intended to serve as the basis of the legal code of an Islamic community. Contrary to what one might expect, the number of states recognizing the *shari'a* as the basis of secular legislation is now greater than it was at the time of the signing of the Universal Declaration of Human Rights and appears to be on the increase. To such states, certain provisions of the Declaration—notably the provision establishing freedom of religion—represent a direct challenge to the basis of their regimes, as was made clear by the Saudis, for example, in justifying their abstention on the vote for the Declaration in 1948. This is by no means to say that Islamic states necessarily engage in persecution of other religions, only that official toleration of religious minorities is a matter of grace rather than right for them.

As regards the question of morality, many Third World states—including many that do not have an established religion, such as Singapore or Taiwan—object to liberal interpretations of human rights that would deny to governments the power to regulate the morals of their citizenry through censorship and other restrictions on public expression and action. It is often difficult for sophisticated observers in the West to appreciate the extent to which concerns of this sort are serious and genuine and not mere excuses for political repression or neurotic manifestations of a residual puritanism.

Establishing Priorities Among Rights

The preceding observations could seem to lend support to the view that human rights should be jettisoned entirely as a factor in U.S. policy toward the Third World. The case for that view would be strong indeed, if it were true that human rights are essentially and inescapably tied to liberal capitalism or to the Western political tradition alone. Yet, as was mentioned earlier, the U.S. pursuit of human rights, with all the parochialism with which it may be charged, has nevertheless had a substantial impact throughout the world, and Third World regimes have shown a sensitivity to human rights complaints—even in instances where they have disregarded them—that is in some cases quite surprising. Much of the reason for this is surely that there is a very large area of agreement between the various international documents on human rights and moral or legal standards that are widely recognized in the religion, traditions, and customs of non-Western societies. If this analysis is correct, it would seem that a successful human rights policy should base itself as much as possible on those aspects of human rights that are most widely acknowledged in the religions and cultures of the Third World and least dependent on conceptions peculiar to Western liberalism.

It is essential, then, that a serious effort be made to distinguish between categories of human rights, rather than embracing indiscriminately everything that has been recognized as a right in some United Nations document. That an order of priorities among rights should be established as part of a human rights policy has generally been understood: If the right not to be tortured or enslaved is put on an equal footing with the right to enjoy paid vacations, as is regularly done in human rights documents, the effect is necessarily to compromise opposition to torture and slavery. Yet systematic attempts to establish such priorities have rarely been made.

In what is generally taken as the most authoritative statement of U.S. policy during the Carter administration, Secretary of State Cyrus Vance's Law Day speech of 1977, three broad categories of human rights are distinguished: 1) "the right to be free from governmental violation of the integrity of the person" (this category was said to "include" torture, cruel forms of punishment, arbitrary arrest and imprisonment, denial of a fair trial, and "invasion of the home"); 2) "the right of the fulfillment of such vital needs as food, shelter, health care, and education"; and 3) "the right to enjoy civil and political liberties—freedom of thought, of religion, of assembly; freedom of speech, freedom of the press; freedom of movement both within and outside one's own country; freedom to take part in government." Secretary Vance gave no indication, however, of the basis of this classification, did not make clear its relation to existing international documents, and made no attempt to distinguish priorities within or among the categories.

That the Vance statement is in crucial respects singularly inept is not difficult to show. By providing a formulation of civil and political liberties that clearly fits, and that seems intended to fit, only liberal democracies in the Western mold, it declares ideological war against the Third World as well as against the Communists. Yet by proceeding to recognize the legitimacy of the "economic and social rights" championed by the international Left and by many in the Third World, it in effect signals capitulation at the outset. For in the event that civil and political rights come into conflict with economic and social rights, as they are bound to do, no reason beyond ideological preference is given for choosing the former over the latter. Moreover, if civil and political rights can legitimately give way to economic and social rights, why should the same not be true of those rights that concern the "integrity of the person"? Is this too not an ideological imposition deriving from the individualist bias of Western liberalism?

In any effort to bring order to this confusion, the first step must be the disestablishment of economic and social rights. If U.S. policymakers cannot agree on the elementary point that there are human rights whose violation is not excused by considerations of an economic or social order, it is better to have no human rights policy at all. This is not to say that the United States should not be sympathetic to the economic and social problems of other nations or should take no account of the impact of economic and social factors on the observance of human rights. It is merely to recognize that needs of this sort cannot be usefully understood as human rights. A government can guarantee to its citizens freedom from arbitrary arrest or the right to vote; it cannot guarantee to its citizens a particular level of nutrition, health care, or education, simply because it is beyond the power of any government to guarantee such things. The Reagan administration has indicated clearly, if unemphatically, its acceptance of this approach.[7]

At the same time, there is undeniable force to the argument that considerations of an economic and social order can under certain circumstances justify the suspension or violation of *some* human rights. If it is nearly impossible to imagine circumstances under which a famine, for example, could justify arbitrary arrest, it is less difficult to imagine circumstances under which it could justify the abrogation of certain property rights or of the right to vote. Accordingly, what seems to be required in the second instance is a redefinition of human rights that purges them of specifically liberal, democratic, and capitalist elements. For to the extent that human rights altogether can be understood merely as a creature of liberal democratic or capitalist ideology, the disestablishment of economic and social rights will appear arbitrary and politically motivated.

Toward a Nonliberal Redefinition of Human Rights

Such a redefinition would seem to require two things. First, a distinction between political rights and civil rights should be made, and political rights should be clearly relegated to a separate status. Political rights—the rights appearing, for example, in Article XXI of the Universal Declaration—can only be exercised in a representative democracy. Civil rights—the rights enumerated, for example, in Articles III–XX of the Universal Declaration—can be exercised under any form of government that conducts itself in accordance with the rule of law. Political rights are thus tied inescapably to liberal democracy in the Western mold, while civil rights are more nearly neutral with respect to forms of government. Centering human rights policy on civil rather than political rights is therefore essential to the extent that the United States wishes to avoid the appearance of ideological crusading on behalf of its own political system.

Yet it is necessary to go one step further. Civil rights as they have been formulated in most human rights documents are only more nearly neutral with respect to forms of government than political rights; they are not neutral simply. Rather, they reflect to a substantial degree the interpretations of civil rights that prevail under liberal political systems and particularly under the American system. In his Law Day speech, Secretary Vance chose to make a distinction between basic civil rights such as freedom from torture and arbitrary arrest and what one may call liberal civil rights—freedom of religion, of speech, and of the press. In doing so, he reflected (and probably intended to appeal to) the specifically American understanding of civil rights in terms of the Bill of Rights of the Constitution. Yet precisely the opposite course should have been followed. Civil rights should be redefined in terms of the principles that are most broadly recognized in a variety of contemporary regimes, and specifically liberal formulations should be avoided or suitably qualified.

To consider in detail how this could be done is beyond the scope of the present discussion, but certain guidelines may be suggested. As was indicated earlier, U.S. views on such matters as separation of church and state and freedom of speech are offensive to governments of very varied political orientations and for reasons that are not always bad. When it is recalled that there are significant disagreements on these matters within the United States itself and between the United States and other advanced democracies (consider, for example, the differences with respect to governmental control of television), the inappropriateness of U.S. dogmatizing in this area becomes evident. This is not to say that such things should not be recognized or championed at all, but merely that a certain range of reasonable restrictions on them should be seen as unobjectionable. In fact, a qualification of just this kind is to be found in more recent international documents,[8] and something like it deserves to be incorporated into U.S. policy statements on human rights.

A similar approach should be taken to the question of property rights. Although the Universal Declaration recognizes a right to private ownership of property, this need not, and should not, be treated as an endorsement of free enterprise capitalism. To link human rights directly to a liberal economic system is as fatal an error as tying them directly to a liberal political system. The argument may be made that civil rights are best guaranteed in a society with an economic system that respects the free choice of individuals, but it should be acknowledged that this condition may be satisfied to some extent under a variety of economic regimes. Considering the mixed nature of most Western economies, this too is a question on which the United States is not in a good position to dogmatize.

One other possible feature of a new human rights policy deserving of consideration particularly in a Third World context is an emphasis on collective or group rights.[9] A serious though largely unremarked failing of past U.S. human rights policy has been its concentration on the treatment of individual dissidents at the expense of persecuted minority groups. This curious myopia almost certainly weakens the credibility and limits the appeal of U.S. policy, particularly in the Third World where persecuted individuals are more apt to be popularly regarded as troublemakers who deserve their fate than as culture heroes. In addition, it obscures the vital distinction between mildly authoritarian regimes engaged in persecuting a few opposition politicians (South Korea, for example) and regimes that habitually discriminate against entire segments of their populations (South Africa or the Soviet Union). Clearly, such an approach would court the danger of appearing to depreciate individual rights and to support any scheme of group entitlements (with attendant implications for the domestic debate over affirmative action). An emphasis on group rights could, however, provide an alternative notion of political rights more universally acceptable than the liberal notion, with its implicit insistence on the principle of "one man, one vote." That is to say, it could be used to provide a test of essential political justice in a regime without requiring a passing of judgment against the political system as such.[10]

The chief advantage of an approach of the sort just outlined is that it establishes a principled basis for distinguishing between moderate and extreme authoritarianism in the Third World. It allows the United States to oppose on human rights grounds genuinely tyrannical regimes, while tolerating or even supporting authoritarian regimes in cases where local conditions make liberal or popular government impracticable. There are some who regard this kind of distinction as insubstantial and a mere rationalization for U.S. support for friendly right-wing dictatorships. Such persons are invited to consider the differences between daily life in Franco's Spain or Park's South Korea and daily life in Idi Amin's Uganda or Pol Pot's Cambodia. These differences are very real indeed for the people who must experience them, and to fail to take account of them is both morally obtuse and politically disadvantageous. It risks turning U.S. human rights policy into an instrument for transforming defective regimes that depend on U.S. support into at least equally imperfect regimes that are in addition hostile to U.S. interests. Transformations of this kind might be thought to be compatible with a commitment to human rights if it were really the case that revolutionary upheaval is a necessary and sufficient condition for the achievement of "economic and social rights." In fact, this claim, so frequently heard from the spokesmen of the international Left in the Third World and so often taken as axiomatic in intellectual circles in the West, is demonstrably fraudulent and should be exposed as such by those responsible for articulating U.S. policy. U.S. spokesmen should be tireless in arguing that the best guarantee of economic and social progress is a political system that guarantees civil rights and a reasonable degree of economic freedom and that these conditions are more likely to be realized under a moderate authoritarian government than under a revolutionary regime professing some variety of socialism.

To what extent authoritarian institutions or measures are justified by local conditions is a question that will never be susceptible to formulaic answers. There may well be circumstances under which very harsh repression may be justified by considerations of national security; in other cases, relatively mild forms of persecution may have no color of necessity. Regimes threatened by terrorism or incipient civil war cannot be held to the same standards with respect to the observance of civil rights as other regimes; but this does not mean that they should be granted a blanket indulgence for declaring war against the political opposition. In each case, a careful and impartial investigation of the factual circumstances should be undertaken before the United States commits itself to a public position on a particular regime.

The Need for Flexibility

At this point it will be convenient to consider the question of U.S. human rights policy toward the Soviet Union and the Communist world generally. Is the solution that is desirable for the Third World also appropriate in the case of the Second? At first glance, a human rights policy that finds itself unable to oppose Communist regimes as undemocratic would seem to be deprived of its most potent weapon. Yet it is one thing to criticize the absence of democracy in a country like Czechoslovakia, with its advanced economy and democratic traditions, and another to criticize its absence in Albania, Outer Mongolia, or, indeed, the Soviet Union. Dissident elements within the Soviet Union and in the emigré community are far from united in a desire to see the current regime replaced by liberal democracy in the Western manner; certainly a very sizable minority tends instead to accept the necessity of an authoritarian government of some sort for the indefinite future. A human rights stance centering on the absence or the precariousness of civil rights in the Soviet Union would appear much better calculated to appeal widely to all segments of the Soviet population. Care should be taken, however, to avoid the blunders of the Carter administration in this area. Concentration on the plight of a few dissident intellectuals tends to convey the impression that the human rights situation in the Soviet Union generally is comparable to that of Third World authoritarian regimes that engage in occasional persecution of politically obnoxious individuals. Lost from sight is the vast qualitative difference between regimes of this sort—which frequently resort to such persecution out of weakness and insecurity—and the Soviet system, with its vast network of labor camps still in operation, its omnipresent secret police, and its methodical persecution of ethnic and religious minority groups. When such things are taken into account, there can be no difficulty in singling out the Soviet Union for opprobrium on the basis of the understanding of human rights suggested above.

Of equal importance is the case of China. Unless the entente between the United States and the People's Republic of China is to constitute a glaring exception to the entire U.S. human rights effort, there must be some latitude in U.S. policy for distinguishing between more and less repressive Communist regimes. The fact that the Chinese have made serious efforts in the last few years to restore the rule of law after the disorders of the Cultural Revolution and to improve their treatment of religious and ethnic minorities (in particular the Tibetans) must go a considerable way toward making the current Chinese regime an acceptable diplomatic associate of this country. A similar argument may be made for a special U.S. relationship with Yugoslavia. The flexibility provided by a human rights policy that is not circumscribed by liberal and capitalist doctrines will prove at least as useful in dealing with the Second World as with the Third. What is more, this ideological neutrality is bound to enhance the credibility of the policy with the populations of Communist states and to make it a more difficult target of official propaganda. Its rhetorical effectiveness will in any case be vastly increased by incorporating the position that violations of fundamental human rights cannot be justified by appeal to economic and social goals.

Whether or to what extent some notion of political rights should continue to be an operational part of U.S. human rights policy is a question that needs to be carefully considered. Obviously, the United States cannot adopt a posture of indifference to the fate of democratic political institutions, and its declaratory policy should leave no doubt of its conviction of the superiority of a liberal and democratic form of government. The question is rather to what extent a failure to adopt or maintain democratic institutions ought to be considered actionable by the United States on human rights grounds. Here, too, not enough attention has been given to the meaning of political rights and the possibility of defining them in such a way as to legitimize a broader range of political institutions than those characteristic of Western liberal democracies. In any event, it makes little sense to insist on understanding political rights dogmatically in terms of election on a basis of "one man, one vote," because not even the United States recognizes this principle as simply valid. Constitutional schemes that grant disproportionate representation to certain groups for political reasons (Zimbabwe, for example, or Fiji) should certainly not be penalized. One might also argue that the same should be true of regimes with political institutions that are tolerably representative or enjoy wide legitimacy but that are not chosen through popular election in a recognizably Western sense of that term. On the other hand, care has to be exercised not to blur the distinctiveness of genuinely free or republican political orders. Above all, no countenance should be given to the claim of regimes of the Left to satisfy the requirement of popular "participation" through mobilization from above.

The difficulties and hazards involved in any such approach could lead to the conclusion, however, that it is better to exclude political rights altogether from the pale of human rights and to regard them, like economic and social rights, as aspirations rather than rights properly speaking. To take this position is not necessarily to write off the possibility of political progress, any more than of economic and social development, or to refuse to provide U.S. assistance in support of it. Indeed, it is entirely compatible with a vigorous program of official support for political democracy and democratic institutions abroad, of the sort announced by President Reagan in his London speech on 8 June 1982. Although such an effort is not without risk, if properly conceived and implemented it is likely to appear less interventionist than a policy of imposing human-rights-related penalties on a regime not for any specific acts but simply for being what it is.

Finally, there is the question of the domestic impact of a human rights policy structured along the lines suggested here. Precisely because of its neutrality in questions of economic and political ideology that continue to agitate U.S. politics, such a policy would seem to provide a basis for constructing the new domestic consensus on foreign policy that the United States badly needs. A policy of the sort proposed would be neither isolationist nor interventionist. It would satisfy the need of most Americans for a sense of idealism and mission in the world and yet not encourage an ideological crusade fraught with various attendant dangers. Consonant with our Vietnam experience, such a policy would reflect awareness of the limits of U.S. power and of the limitations of liberal democracy as a political model for all nations regardless of their historical experience or political culture. At the same time, it would not have us retreat to a posture of *realpolitik* based on a simple cultural relativism or to a complacent cultivation of our own garden. Clearly, there can be no guarantee that such a policy will prove immediately popular in every instance, and it is probably inevitable that U.S. support of Third World autocrats will encounter substantial domestic criticism. Much may certainly be accomplished, however, by a forthright presentation and reasoned defense of official views and actions. The vaporous rhetoric that has substituted for thought and policy in the past, and that has so frequently been given the lie by the hard business of dealing with international realities, has probably done almost as much to discredit human rights policy at home as it has abroad. There is every reason to believe that the political understanding of the American people in foreign affairs has been as consistently underestimated by its own recent leadership as have been its qualities of resolution and will.

Notes

1. Elizabeth Drew, "Human Rights," *New Yorker,* 18 July 1977, p. 36.

2. For an account of the persisting intellectual confusion on this subject, see Myres S. McDougal, Harold D. Lasswell, and Lung-chu Chen, *Human Rights and World Public Order* (New Haven/London: Yale University Press, 1980), pp. 63–82.

3. For an elaboration of this view, see, for example, Adamantia Pollis and Peter Schwab, eds., *Human Rights: Cultural and Ideological Perspectives* (New York: Praeger, 1980).

4. Daniel P. Moynihan, "The United States in Opposition," *Commentary* 59 (March 1975): 31–44.

5. The extent to which this assumption acquired the character of dogma in U.S. official as well as academic thinking has been documented by Robert A. Packenham, *Liberal America and the Third World* (Princeton: Princeton University Press, 1973).

6. A good discussion of this insufficiently appreciated point may be found in Walter Berns, *The First Amendment and the Future of American Democracy* (New York: Basic Books, 1976), pp. 1–32.

7. See. U.S. Department of State, *Country Reports on Human Rights Practices for 1981* (Washington, D.C.: U.S. Government Printing Office, 1982), pp. 1–11.

8. In the United Nations International Covenant on Civil and Political Rights (1966), the rights of speech, assembly, and association are to be subject to such restrictions as are "necessary in a democratic society in the interests of national security or public safety, public order (*ordre public*), the protection of public health or morals or the protection of the rights and freedoms of others."

9. See Vernon Van Dyke, "The Individual, the State and Ethnic Communities in Political Theory," in Donald P. Kommers and Gilburt D. Loescher, eds., *Human Rights and American Foreign Policy* (South Bend, Ind.: University of Notre Dame Press, 1979), pp. 36–62.

10. The case of South Africa is of particular interest in this respect. The approach just suggested makes it possible for the United States to oppose the policy of apartheid in its current form without supporting a political system based on "one man, one vote" (which is to say, given current and foreseeable circumstances, a black revolution). The new constitution of Zimbabwe shows how group rights of whites and blacks can be respected while preserving a (politically essential) numerical asymmetry.

8

Conclusion

Human Rights Abroad and at Home

James H. Nichols, Jr.

Since the time of the ancient Greek writers, at least, citizens, statesmen, and political thinkers have debated what place considerations of justice should have in foreign affairs. In modern times—let us say since the seventeenth century—political justice in the most influential version has been understood in terms of rights. This characteristically modern understanding is exemplified with outstanding clarity in our own Declaration of Independence: Moved by a decent respect to the opinions of mankind, the authors of American independence sought to demonstrate the justice of their action by appealing to fundamental principles of human rights and their political consequences. The contemporary issue of the role that considerations of human rights should play in the conduct of our foreign policy is the most frequent form assumed today by the perennial question concerning the place of justice in international politics.

All the authors of the preceding essays would agree, I believe, with Aristotle's cogent argument that a country's foreign relations must be conducted with a view to principles of justice.[1] Citizens and their leaders do, of course, often choose to act unjustly toward foreigners and foreign countries in a manner that they would find evidently unacceptable among themselves, and the immediate advantages of such injustice are usually quite obvious. In the long run, however, unjust foreign policy is likely to harm domestic political life; through often impressive examples, it teaches citizens general disrespect for justice and thus subverts the moral foundations of decent politics at home. The relation between domestic and foreign politics is complex: On the one hand, most people do make commonsense distinctions between the principles of action (obligation, justice, trust) that are appropriate to the two separate realms; but on the other hand, the principles of action in one realm tend to penetrate into the other.

Aristotle rejected as unsound the sort of *realpolitik* in foreign affairs that would treat justice as irrelevant and insubstantial. Such a view of *realpolitik* had been given a classic formulation in the pages of Thucydides' *Peloponnesian War*.[2] Ambassadors from democratic Athens tried to persuade the leaders of the small island of Melos to yield to the demand that they become tributary subjects of the Athenian Empire. Although these Athenian leaders conceded that justice may have some application to the relations between rough equals in power, they denied that considerations of justice have any proper place in relations between strong and weak. In using compulsion and rejecting any appeal to justice, the Athenians claimed to act in accord with nature and in a manner deserving of no blame. It would be foolish of the Melians, they argued, to rely on the empty hope that justice would prevail, for example, through divine support for justice. The Melians, however, under the influence of hope and perhaps a sense of honor, refused to yield to these arguments; they eventually suffered the disaster of being conquered by Athens. At first sight, the outcome might seem to support the kind of *realpolitik* articulated by the Athenian ambassadors; but in the larger context of events narrated by Thucydides, the view later formulated by Aristotle is upheld. Injustice as displayed by those Athenian leaders ultimately destroyed Athens: Leaders after Pericles tended to seek their private advantage rather than the common good of the country, and the people became filled with such a distrust of their leaders that they would no longer confide adequate power to those most competent to conduct their affairs successfully.[3]

None of the authors of the preceding essays seems to accept the *realpolitik* expressed by those Athenian ambassadors; indeed, virtually no Americans today do so. On this point some historical perspective helps, such as the articles by Abram N. Shulsky and Charles H. Fairbanks, Jr., provide. Even self-proclaimed advocates of *realpolitik* tend today to take for granted elements of a moral horizon that was not fashioned by *realpolitik* alone. As Fairbanks points out, today's proponents of *realpolitik* tend not to consider seriously—let alone to recommend —convening international conferences in order to slaughter all the participants at once. Likewise, Americans partial to *realpolitik* do not, I think, consider seriously doing the kinds of things done by the Athenians: seeking a small country's submission to our imperial rule and, failing that, conquering the country, slaughtering all adult males, and selling women and children into slavery. If Socrates' suggestion that justice is tameness (or gentleness) as opposed to wildness (or savagery) is correct,[4] it seems that Americans—and indeed, other citizens of liberal democracies today—are more just than the Athenian democrats of old in their dispositions and actions toward foreign affairs.

The people of the United States have a deeply-rooted sense of what Aristotle points out: One cannot maintain a total and absolute separation between the principles by which a country acts abroad and the principles by which it conducts its political life at home. In a prephilosophic world, such a separation could no doubt be maintained by a society convinced that foreigners were wholly alien, beings of another species for all practical purposes. But for Aristotle such a separation was irrational and untenable, and it is still more obviously so for Americans, whose fundamental principles of political justice, as expressed in the Declaration of Independence, rest on "an abstract truth, applicable to all men and all times."[5] These same principles that proclaim that legitimate government rests on the consent of human beings equally endowed with inalienable rights also teach that it is wrong for a country to seek by force to impose its imperial will on others. In fact, the vast majority of citizens in liberal democracies hold that considerations of justice should figure at least to this extent in the conduct of foreign affairs. This shared conviction, of course, underlies the fact that no two liberal democracies have ever gone to war with each other and the hope that the spread of liberal democracy would make the world more peaceful. By contrast, the Soviet claim that the extension by force of its rule (or the imposition by force of its kind of regime) advances mankind toward the final solution of all economic, political, and social problems involves the rejection of any restraints imposed by justice on actions in foreign affairs; it thus arouses reasonable fear in those against whom warlike action might be directed.

Let us restate this point of liberal democratic agreement—that our foreign policy must take account of justice—in the modern language of rights: As our own political community rests on the recognition of human rights and seeks to secure them, so our foreign policy must respect the rights of others. Most basically, we must therefore refrain from unjust conquests; we must not try to enslave or rob others or to violate international agreements to which we are a party. To most Americans, I think, these and similar obligations do not seem unduly burdensome; they are willing to respect others' rights provided only that others reciprocate. In our age of utopian demands, these moral obligations may not seem impressively lofty, but—viewed in historical perspective—this degree of acceptance by popular opinion of justice in international affairs represents a remarkable achievement of political morality.

Promoting the Rights of Other Peoples

Differences begin to arise, however, on the question of what our government should do about foreigners whose rights are violated by their own governments or by foreign domination. As the article by

Clifford Orwin and Thomas Pangle makes clear, a theoretical argument may be made for little or no activity on behalf of the rights of others: If sovereign states are in a state of nature with each other, one country may be obligated to act justly toward others but not to be concerned with another government's actions toward its own citizens. But in fact Americans are traditionally not indifferent to the human rights of others. The universalism of fundamental principles that I have already mentioned as expressed in the Declaration of Independence guarantees, for as long as those principles remain the vital core of American political opinion, that Americans will hope that others too will be able to secure their human rights. This hope springs from a twofold motivation: self-interest and benevolence toward our fellow man. Americans consider foreign governments that secure their own citizens' rights more likely to be peaceful members of the international order and, if need be, allies. But at the same time, with the recognition of their common humanity, Americans wish that others might enjoy the same blessings of liberty. This impulse of benevolence is strengthened by a development in American political thinking succinctly stated by Shulsky in chapter 2. The liberating Enlightenment doctrine of natural rights, state of nature, and contract

> combined with older elements of the Western tradition, stemming from classical antiquity and the revealed religions, to produce a belief in the value of human freedom, not only as an efficacious and profitable organizing principle for society, but ultimately as something worth more than prosperity, security, or life itself.

What can be done to advance the cause of human rights worldwide? An enduring theme in U.S. politics is that our successful example is the most powerful—as it is surely the least problematic—way in which to encourage the respect for human rights abroad. Ten days before his death at the age of eighty-three, Thomas Jefferson wrote of the decision to declare independence:

> May it be to the world, what I believe it will be (to some parts sooner, to others later, but finally to all), the signal of arousing men to burst the chains under which monkish ignorance and superstition had persuaded them to bind themselves, and to assume the blessings and security of self-government. That form which we have substituted, restores the free right to the unbounded exercise of reason and freedom of opinion. All eyes are opened, or opening, to the rights of man.[6]

This vigorous and confident statement looks to universal progress in securing human rights, inspired by the signal example of the United States. When Myron Rush writes (in chapter 5) that "probably the United States can best encourage progressive developments in the USSR by cultivating its own inner strengths and by resisting Soviet expansionism," he adapts that same basic Jeffersonian strategy to our situation in regard to the most powerful opponent of human rights today.

Can we do something to favor the cause of human rights beyond being an example worthy of imitation? A country's capacity to act for human rights clearly depends on its overall power and place in the international order and the consequent room for maneuver that it enjoys. Toward one extreme, we may consider the case of Great Britain in the nineteenth century. Fairbanks shows that Great Britain's political strength and economic and naval preeminence were crucial conditions of her capacity to carry out a successful interventionist human rights campaign against the slave trade. Toward the other extreme, we may consider Great Britain in 1941: Faced with the direst necessities of survival, Churchill had no room for maneuver on human rights issues; he could not possibly reject alliance with Stalin's Soviet Union, however horrendous were the latter's violations of human rights.

In the nineteenth century, the United States was too weak on the world scene to think seriously of positive action on behalf of human rights; furthermore, the nation's moral, political, and ultimately military energies were quite fully engaged in the struggle to put an end to our own most grievous violation of human rights, the institution of chattel slavery. Great Britain, not the United States, had the power and confidence to act on behalf of human rights on the world scene. Jefferson, and later Lincoln, could nonetheless entertain high hopes for the spread of human rights and self-government through the ultimate power of the U.S. example, and the course of events seemed to be moving in this direction. As Shulsky suggests, however, the twentieth century is different: Modern tyranny clothed in totalitarian ideology poses a more threatening, and perhaps still growing, challenge to human rights; in this context, the United States may arguably need to do more on behalf of human rights than in the nineteenth century. Certainly we have more power and preeminence than we did then; but we do not enjoy the degree of effective preeminence of nineteenth-century Great Britain.

If we do not approach one extreme as closely as Great Britain in the nineteenth century, how closely do we approach the other extreme—a situation of dire necessity? Rush seems to locate us somewhat closer to this situation than the other contributors do and hence to reason that our geopolitical position leaves us less leeway for worldwide actions in favor of human rights. He even draws a parallel between our moving toward despotic China in the last decade and our necessity to ally with Stalin in 1941. (In this connection, we may feel pleased by Chinese efforts toward improvement in some aspects of human rights, mentioned in Carnes Lord's article; but this does not fundamentally affect Rush's point.) Rush's article requires us constantly to hold in view the Soviet Union's great military power and its ruthlessness in suppressing opposition to official lines of policy and opinion, in the USSR and in East Europe, whether that opposition is expressed in the name of human rights or of anything else. From this perspective Rush doubts that greater benefits than costs would effectively emerge from our making a global commitment to human rights the central thrust of our foreign policy.

Whether or not we finally accept Rush's judgment on the potential costs and benefits of human rights policy, we must, I think, welcome the clarity of several important distinctions that he makes. The discussion of human rights policy has too frequently been an area of good feelings rather than a chain of lucid argument. Rush's analysis of the several proximate goals, at least partly conflicting, at which human rights policy could aim, of the various means best suited to these goals, and of the different corresponding views of Soviet reality brings powerfully to the fore clear issues with which any rational human rights policy must come to grips.

Western Principles and Non-Western Societies

James Ring Adams is more hopeful concerning what U.S. human rights policy may do; he detects some grounds to believe that it has achieved something of value through the Helsinki process. The achievement is to be found, Adams argues, not in geopolitical gains nor, for that matter, in better treatment of dissidents by the Soviet Union, but in the area of "intangibles." The West has managed to work together to formulate, and to win Soviet acceptance of, an international agreement in which a basically Western understanding of human rights is embodied. This Helsinki document is better, from the standpoint of a true understanding of human rights, than various recent United Nations documents, where various overextensions and corruptions of genuine human rights run rampant. Its value is enhanced by the way it expressly appeals to public opinion and thus serves as a "didactic document"; above all, dissident supporters of human rights in East Europe and in the Soviet Union itself have rallied round the Helsinki standard. No less noteworthy is the effect of all this on American public opinion; as Adams (chapter 6) puts it:

> Americans seemed surprised by the vitality of the overseas appeal of their basic political tradition. The rights embodied in the U.S. Constitution were being eagerly sought by people of evident decency and intelligence who had been thoroughly exposed to Communist doctrine and practice. In retrospect, this period marked a watershed from the self-doubt of the Vietnam War.

It has often been noted that foreign wars may serve to unify and energize domestic political opinion; here we have the example of a comparable domestic effect from a peaceful campaign on behalf of human rights. It is often said that the appeal to human rights may build domestic consensus for our foreign policy; here it appears that human rights policy abroad could also serve to revivify American awareness of the value of their political principles at home.

Whereas Adams considers the clearly Western character displayed in the human rights aspects of the Helsinki document to be a definite boon, Lord tries to articulate a human rights policy as free as possible of specifically Western, liberal, capitalist elements. The most important advantage that this particular approach seems to seek to achieve would be to lessen the costs of conducting a human rights policy by centering that policy on the most broadly recognized rights—rights that figure not only in political philosophies of the West but in many other religions, ethical traditions, and political cultures. By concentrating on such rights, we could condemn the more hideous tyrants while not offending more decent autocrats of various stripes; our policy could be applied universally and consistently; and we could stand up for some basic human rights without alienating ourselves from the multitudinous countries that in various ways differ from, and cannot or do not wish to emulate, Western liberal democracies.

These are attractive advantages for our human rights policy, and surely we must strive suitably to adapt the application of ideas of human rights as they have developed in specific details among us to the immense variety of non-Western societies. I cannot help fearing, however, that Lord's proposal, in seeking to avoid specifically Western elements, becomes minimalist in its effort to be universalist, that it goes too far toward discarding what is most fundamental and most inspiring in our understanding and practice of human rights. On the one hand, Lord would move our human rights policy away from a distinctively liberal individualist basis; he even entertains the possibility of an emphasis on collective or group rights. However, as Orwin and Pangle point out, human rights coherently understood belong to human beings as individuals. Something like "group rights," including of course rights of minorities, "are at most the expression of the rights of the individuals who comprise the groups." To lose sight of the individual character of human rights runs the risk of cutting them off from their rational foundation. On the other hand, Lord wants to downplay some specifically liberal rights such as political rights, freedom of religion, and freedom of speech. Let us consider the case of political rights. Surely no sensible person would want us to try to insist that other countries adopt detailed specific features of our political institutions, and certainly many countries are in such circumstances at the present time that they can take no immediate steps toward representative democracy. As Pangle and Orwin put it in their first metaphor, political rights may be viewed as the apex of a pyramid, other rights being more basic. But later they revise the metaphor, I believe rightly, to view political rights as the keystone of the arch. It seems to me that we should want our policy to uphold the whole structure of human rights; even though various countries may not now be in a position to realize this whole, it can stand as an inspiring goal for future attainment. Too much accommodation to existing illiberal conditions in the Third World and elsewhere could deprive a human rights policy of its most vital content. I fear, too, that it could contribute some further confusion to the understanding of human rights at home, which Fred Baumann's article shows to be already too full of obfuscation in some quarters.

Public Opinion and National Security

My remarks on the articles by Rush, Adams, and Lord dealing with human rights policy have up to now brought forth and emphasized their distinctive features and hence differences, but these differences are somewhat less upon closer examination than they appear at first sight. Lord is primarily concerned with a policy of human rights that we would spell out clearly and carry out consistently. But he also recognizes another type of policy, which he calls "declaratory." In the area of declaratory policy, it seems, he would not oppose emphasis on the more demanding and farther-reaching human rights, including political rights, characteristic of representative democracies. Thus the difference between Lord's and Adams's approaches need not be quite so stark as it seemed in the first formulation; and Lord might respond to the reservations I have stated along similar lines. At the same time, however, I suspect that Adams might join me in wondering how great a separation between declaratory human rights policy and universally applied human rights policy is ultimately tenable.

In this connection I must also restate in more precise detail the manner in which Rush passes a generally unfavorable judgment on human rights policy. He does not advise against any action by our government in favor of human rights abroad. In fact, he asserts that our government "should use its influence to discourage immoral practices by governments that depend on us for assistance, while recognizing the necessary limits of our beneficent influence"; he accepts that our government should on occasion denounce especially heinous violations of human rights by Communist governments or try privately to intercede with other governments on behalf of people whose rights are being abused. What his argument attacks is the endeavor to make a global crusade for human rights the centerpiece or the highest priority of our foreign policy. For Rush, "our central concern must be to protect U.S. security and to promote a world in which our democratic way of life will be safe." If, as Rush affirms, "the chief threat to U.S. security emanates from the Soviet-centered Communist movement," and if the United States is the most powerful force supporting human rights in the world today, then even a universalist concern for human rights would require us to make our national security the goal of greatest urgency. Human rights policy, insofar as it aims at other praiseworthy goals, must not be allowed to do any serious damage to the goal of national security.

The other contributors, I believe, would all accept Rush's argument as just sketched. The differences among them do not concern goals or fundamental principles, but turn on differences of emphasis, different weighings of costs and benefits, different judgments of the relative significance of the several factors, domestic as well as foreign, involved in the international situation. How then might one agree with the main lines of Rush's argument and yet end up more hopeful for what an emphasis by our foreign policy on human rights could achieve? Let me give two examples of such different judgments. First, Rush admits that "a case might be made for a global commitment to human rights as providing . . . a moral basis for foreign policy with which to oppose the Communist ideology" but rejects this because of excessive costs. However, a more prudent positioning and application of human rights policy might lessen those costs. We might be justified in placing a heavier weight on the necessity of restoring public consensus and support for a reasonable foreign policy through such a moral basis. We would give all the more weight to this domestic factor the more we judged that public opinion regarding our foreign policy was confused, frag- mented, or demoralized.

Second, Rush concedes that the most effective aspect of Carter's human rights campaign arguably lay in its focusing world attention on Soviet domestic abuses of human rights. "The resulting gains for the United States in the contest for world opinion were not insubstantial, yet they were necessarily limited." In countries where political oppression is practiced, popular favor thus won, if any, is likely to be counterbalanced by antagonism on the part of the government. Concerning other countries, such as NATO members, Rush (chapter 5) argues that

> public opinion is no longer as ignorant as it once was about the nature of the Soviet regime. On the crucial questions for them—how active a threat to their own security is the USSR and what sacrifices are required to deal with this threat?—focusing attention on the Soviet government's persecution of its own people is unlikely to have great effect.

This latter point, I think, is debatable. In one sense, of course, knowledge of the Soviet regime is indeed available, but I suspect that Rush overestimates the effective availability and clarity of such knowledge in European and U.S. public opinion.[7] Strong considerations work together to make people eager to see the Soviet reality as different from what it really is. Shulsky points out that convergence theories, in a rather straightforward manner, and, more subtly, a new central emphasis on "global" or "North-South" issues, seek to bridge the ideological gap, that is, to show the Soviet regime to be not fundamentally different from ours. In consequence, continual efforts must arguably be made to keep Western publics aware of the character of the threat and thus willing to make the sacrifices necessary to counter it. This necessity is all the greater if neutralism in Europe—what Walter Laqueur has recently called "Hollanditis"—is on the upswing.[8] From this perspective, human rights policy might have a more crucial role to play than Rush grants it. I would like to conclude this argument on a note with which, I believe, all the contributors would concur: This use of human rights policy must be prudently carried out with special care not to mislead public opinion into thinking that the crucial goals of foreign policy can be achieved by human rights rhetoric alone.

Attaining and Preserving Human Rights

Whatever character and order of rank human rights policy should have in the conduct of our foreign affairs, we shall certainly be less able to promote human rights, abroad or at home, if we lack a rational, defensible, and clear understanding of what they are. The articles by Pangle and Orwin and by Baumann accomplish a valuable service by presenting the sort of clear and coherent understanding that is needed and by defending human rights thus understood against a multitude of incoherent extensions, odd excrescences, and even downright reversals. Drawing on the wealth of their arguments, I should like to conclude this essay by discussing three aspects of human rights; their simplicity, their practicability, and the efforts that are needed to preserve them.

First, I would argue that the basic doctrine of human rights was originally formulated to be, is, and of right ought to remain, simple. Once more, the Declaration of Independence adequately illustrates this point. It does not elaborate what all the human rights are, but it states briefly and clearly the most fundamental rights and the basic reasoning upon which the whole doctrine of rights rests. Jefferson's famous letter describes the object of the Declaration thus:

> To place before mankind the common sense of the subject, in terms so plain and firm as to command their assent, and to justify ourselves in the independent stand we are compelled to take. Neither aiming at originality of principle or sentiment, nor yet copied from any particular and previous writing, it was intended to be an expression of the American mind, and to give to that expression the proper tone and spirit called for by the occasion. All its authority rests then on the harmonizing sentiments of the day, whether expressed in conversation, in letters, printed essays, or in the elementary books of public right, as Aristotle, Cicero, Locke, Sidney, etc.[9]

The Declaration was thus intended to be a political document clearly comprehensible to most ordinary political men. To understand it required, to be sure, some degree of political literacy and experience, but not advanced, sophisticated learning. It is simple and straightforward in just the way that its correlates—equal protection of the laws and equal opportunity—are, in contrast with the complicated justifications of quotas and unequal treatment for the sake of equality of results, whose tortuous paths of academic and bureaucratic reasoning are explicated by Baumann.

To avoid misunderstanding I must qualify—that is, complicate—my simple assertion about the simplicity of the basic doctrine of human rights in two ways. I by no means wish to deny that securing human rights in actual political practice involves countless complexities. One right will often conflict with another; some generally respected right may conflict with some urgent political necessity; the limits to which a right can be reasonably extended may be doubtful—numerous reasonable Supreme Court decisions (not to mention the quirkier ones) wrestle with these kinds of real complexities. Nor do I wish to deny that complicated philosophical issues surround the doctrine of human rights. A complete theoretical defense of human rights would have to investigate the great alternative ways of thinking about nature, man, and politics; to explore the original distinctive insights and purposes that led to the formulation of a doctrine of human rights; to inquire into the several variations of the human rights doctrine from its origin to the present; to decide what version of human rights is most convincing (which could, of course, turn out to be a newly developed variant); and to persuade us that the doctrine thus presented is in fact superior to the alternatives. The articles by Baumann and by Pangle and Orwin enable us to get a good sense of these complexities. Indeed, by looking again at the passage quoted from Jefferson's letter, we may gain insight into the difficult issues that were already involved, even before the doctrine of human rights was transformed by the theories of Rousseau, Kant, and Hegel. If the Declaration formulates a common agreement by Americans on political principle to be found somehow expressed in contemporary communications—and also in Aristotle, Cicero, Locke, and Sidney—surely a theoretical argument of some sophistication would be needed fully to make sense of this. Yet Jefferson's assertion about the Declaration—that it presents the common sense of the subject in plain terms and is an expression of the American mind—is nonetheless persuasive and adequately points out the inherent simplicity of the basic doctrine of human rights.

As to the practicability of human rights, I would maintain that the securing of human rights is a moderate and attainable goal. Everyone, I think, senses that this goal is not easy; an important range of preconditions must doubtless be available to a political society if it is to do a good job of securing human rights. Political scientists have long debated and will continue to debate what those preconditions are; it seems likely that they include a fairly high level of literacy and enlightenment, a substantial degree of moral consensus (which in practice probably rests most firmly on a religious basis), and—what is most debated—some degree of favorable material and economic conditions. The point is that the goal, though not easy, is not utopian. It does not require a radical change in human nature: that men become angels, or philosophers, or new socialist men. Nor does it require the complete conquest or overcoming of nature—so as, for example, forever to eliminate scarcity. Not only is it not utopian, it is not even the most difficult imaginable nonutopian goal: The best regime elaborated by Aristotle and the fully legitimate democratic society envisioned by Rousseau both require a fuller and less likely list of preconditions for their achievement. Somewhere between easy and utopian, the goal of securing human rights may be substantially achieved if conditions are moderately favorable.

A key notion here is "substantial achievement" in securing human rights, which of course must be distinguished from perfect achievement. Absolute perfection in the securing of human rights—like absolute perfection in anything human—is surely impossible, as can easily be seen. Basic to the security of rights is assurance against violence to one's person. Laws, law enforcement, and criminal justice aim to provide such assurance, but they can never do so perfectly; an all-out attempt to provide perfect assurance would necessarily trample on other rights and harm other goods. Perfect achievement, no; but substantial achievement in the securing of human rights can be attained—and this, of course, to various degrees. For example, it makes sense to say that in 1789 the United States substantially achieved this goal, but one would have to add that the achievement was still grievously flawed by the deprivation of human rights of those black Americans who were slaves. Our substantial achievement of securing human rights today is more complete.

The securing of human rights, thus understood as a substantially attainable goal, is to be contrasted with other kinds of political goals that are unlimited and unattainable, withdrawing from our grasp as we seem to approach them. Of this unlimited sort is the Communist goal of a totally abundant, collectivized, and yet free life with the eventual abolition of politics and its replacement with administration. The goal of equality of results has a similarly, if less evidently, unlimited character. A consequence of such limitless political goals is their tendency to call forth and justify the use of unlimited means to pursue them; and human rights are among the limits over which unlimited, unrestrained political means are sure to run. The result tends to be some form of tyranny. Mao's notion of permanent revolution is a revealing expression of the consequence of devoting a political community to limitless goals. Certain limits, certain restraints on action are by contrast inherent in the idea of respecting and securing human rights.

Does the assertion that the United States has substantially achieved the goal of securing human rights invite us to lapse into contemptible complacency? By no means: As the old maxim that the price of liberty is eternal vigilance suggests, the continued maintaining of human rights requires, not permanent revolution, but ongoing efforts. The task of providing for national defense is never taken care of once and for all.

Domestically, the practical difficulties of striking the best balance among competing rights must be wrestled with every day. Plenty of work is needed for the prudent improvement of the security of rights. The wholehearted commitment to equal protection of the laws and equal opportunity is morally demanding, as Baumann shows, for there are always incentives to cheat; in consequence, he even calls the commitment "fragile." Furthermore, the securing of rights, such as equal protection of the laws, may be our fundamental political goal, but it does not exhaust the range of political tasks. For example, that access to public education should be equal for all is part of the right of equal protection; but to improve the quality of education involves problems beyond that.

A final word on the efforts needed to preserve human rights: Crucial to preserving them is continued awareness of their value and of the value of the political order that secures them. That awareness, it would seem, is too easily forgotten. Indeed, I suspect that if the commitment to human rights is fragile, forgetfulness is principally to blame. This consequence follows partly from the status of human rights themselves: They are crucial to the complete human good but do not guarantee attainment of that good. The individual's rights to life, liberty, and the pursuit of happiness may be secure, but happiness may remain elusive. It becomes easy then to forget how valuable the security of those rights is. We can best be reminded by contemplating the alternative presented by political societies where such rights are regularly violated. Our awareness of the value of human rights has frequently been revitalized by streams of immigrants coming to this country; perhaps a prudent emphasis on human rights in our foreign policy may also contribute something to that revitalization.

Notes

1. Aristotle, *Politics*, Book VII, 1324b, and 1333b–1334a, ed. H. Rackham (Cambridge, Mass.: Loeb Classical Library, Harvard University Press, 1959).

2. Thucydides, *History of the Peloponnesian War*, 4 vols., with an English translation by Charles Foster Smith (Cambridge, Mass.: Loeb Classical Library, Harvard University Press, 1962), vol. 3, Book V, chapters 84–116.

3. See Leo Strauss, *The City and Man* (Chicago: Rand McNally, 1964), pp. 184–209.

4. Plato, *Gorgias*, 516c–d, ed. W.R.M. Lamb (Cambridge, Mass.: Loeb Classical Library, Harvard University Press, 1961).

5. *The Collected Works of Abraham Lincoln*, ed. Roy P. Basler (New Brunswick, N.J.: Rutgers University Press, 1953), vol. 3, p. 376.

6. Thomas Jefferson, Letter to Roger C. Weightman, 24 June 1826, in *Selected Writings*, ed. Harvey C. Mansfield, Jr. (Arlington Heights, Ill.: AHM Publishing Corp., 1979), pp. 12–13.

7. Rush himself, for example, makes a cogent argument against a widely held view of Soviet reality that underlies one aspect of human rights policy. If our policy aims at using rewards and penalties to lead the Soviet government to moderate its treatment of dissidents, this presupposes that the Soviet gov-

ernment uses more oppression than it really needs to. But such a view of the Soviet regime, Rush argues, is probably false.

8. Walter Laqueur, "Hollanditis:—a New Stage in European Neutralism," in *Commentary*, August 1981, pp. 19–26.

9. Jefferson, Letter to Henry Lee, 8 May 1825, in *Selected Writings*, pp. 11–12.

Index